DON'T BELIEVE THE HYPE:

WHEN TRUST IS ON THE LINE – AN EXECUTIVE GUIDE ON KEEPING YOUR BRAND RESILIENT IN THE ERA OF DIGITAL + AI.

GAL BORENSTEIN

Copyright © 2025 by Gal Borenstein.

All rights reserved.

No part of this book may be reproduced, stored in a retrieval system, or transmitted in any form or by any means, electronic, mechanical, photocopying, recording, or otherwise, without the prior written permission of the publisher, except for brief quotations used in reviews or scholarly works.

Printed in United States of America.

Contact the Author: Gal Borenstein, Email: **Gal@BorensteinGroup.com**, Tel: 703-597-1610,

DEDICATION 1

PROLOGUE 3
Who Can You Trust? - There's an Executive Guide for That. 3

PART I: SKEPTICAL MUCH? HOW WE GOT HERE 7

1. Fake Reviews and Fake News - A New Generation of Trust in Danger 8
   Craft Your Leadership Trust Strategy 13
   Steps for the Strategic Leader to Combat Fake Reviews and Fake News: 15

2. Bridging the Trust Gap - From Traditional to Digital Marketing 17
   Craft Your Leadership Trust Strategy 21
   Steps for the Strategic Leader to Bridge the Trust Gap: 22

3. Big Failures in Building Trusted Brands 24
   Craft Your Leadership Trust Strategy: 30
   Steps for the Strategic Leader to Build and Safeguard Brand Trust: 33

PART II: UNDERSTANDING TRUST IN THE DIGITAL AGE 34

4. Borenstein's GUARDIAN Digital Trust Framework™ - Building a Digital Trust Ecosystem 35
   The GUARDIAN Framework in Action 40
   Implementing Borenstein's GUARDIAN Digital Trust Framework™ 51

5. The Top 20 Constructs for Building a Trusted Brand 55
   Practical Constructs and Tactics for Trust Building 57
   Craft Your Leadership Trust Strategy 59
   Steps for the Strategic Leader to Build Trust Constructs: ... 60

6. Trust Hacking and Leveraging Social Proof to Build Brand Loyalty in a Skeptical Digital World 62
    Craft Your Leadership Trust Strategy 66
    Steps for the Strategic Leader for Leveraging Social Proof and UGC Aligned with GUARDIAN Principles: 70

7. Trust and Social Media: Managing Online Reputations in a Distrustful Age 71
    Craft Your Leadership Trust Strategy 76
    Steps for the Strategic Leader to Manage Social Media Trust: 80

8. Why Trust is Becoming Increasingly Crucial in the Digital Age for Brands 82

9. Trust by the Numbers - Core Stats that Define the Trust Economy 86
    Craft Your Leadership Trust Strategy 91
    Steps for the Strategic Leader to Evaluate Core Stats: 92

10. The Main Challenges Businesses Faced Related to the Decline of Trust in 2023 - 2024 94
    Craft Your Leadership Trust Strategy 102
    Steps for the Strategic Leader to Overcome the Main Challenges in Business: 103

11. The Biggest Challenges Marketers Face in Building and Maintaining Trust in the Digital Age 105
    Craft Your Leadership Trust Strategy 110
    Steps for the Strategic Leader to Maintain Digital Trust: . 112

12. What We Trust Depends on the Generation We Come From 114
    Craft Your Leadership Trust Strategy 118
    Steps for the Strategic Leader to Reach Each Generation: 119

PART III: WHAT CAN YOU DO ABOUT IT? 121

13. Building Trust Through Customer Service in the AI Age .. 122
    Craft Your Leadership Trust Strategy 128

Steps For the Strategic Leader to Build Trust Through
Customer Service: 129

14. How Brands Can Balance Authenticity and Storytelling to Gain Trust **131**
Craft Your Leadership Trust Strategy 135
Steps For the Strategic Leader to Balance Authenticity and
Storytelling: 136

15. Communicating Brand Values to Gen-Z: Navigating the Authenticity Imperative **138**
Craft Your Leadership Trust Strategy 144
Steps for the Strategic Leader when Targeting Gen-Z: 146

16. Addressing Security Concerns to Restore Trust in Digital Platforms **148**
Craft Your Leadership Trust Strategy 154
Steps For the Strategic Leader when Addressing Security
Concerns: 157

17. Overcoming Trust Challenges in B2B and B2C Marketing 158
Craft Your Leadership Trust Strategy 167
Steps For the Strategic Leader when Building Trust with B2B
Clients: 170

PART IV: MANAGING TRUST IN CRISIS SITUATIONS
.... 172

18. Trust in Crisis Management **173**
Craft Your Leadership Trust Strategy 178
Steps For the Strategic Leader when Navigating a Crisis: . 180

19. Crisis of Confidence - How to Rebuild Trust After a Major Product Failure **181**
Craft Your Leadership Trust Strategy 187
Steps for the Strategic Leader to Recover from a Product
Failure: 190

20. Effective Crisis Management to Rebuild Trust and Win Back Customers **191**

Craft Your Leadership Trust Strategy 197
Steps For the Strategic Leader to Recover from a Crisis: .. 200

21. Rebuilding Brand Reputation Amidst Internal and External Crisis 202
Craft Your Leadership Trust Strategy 206
Steps for the Strategic Leader to Rebuild Reputation after a PR Crisis: 210

22. Rebuilding Trust After a Digital Crisis or Scandal 212
Craft Your Leadership Trust Strategy 216
Steps for the Strategic Leader to Rebuild Trust: 217

23. Crisis of Trust in Data Management 219
Craft Your Leadership Trust Strategy 222
Steps for the Strategic Leader to Build Trust in Data Management: 225

PART V: LEVERAGING TRUST FOR GROWTH 227

24. Corporate Social Responsibility (CSR) and Brand Purpose in Trust Building 228
Craft Your Leadership Trust Strategy 232
Steps for the Strategic Leader for Developing CSR and Brand Purpose: 237

25. Building Trust Through Strategic Innovation 238
Craft Your Leadership Trust Strategy: 241
Steps for the Strategic Leader to Build Trust through Strategic Innovation: 243

26. Building Trust Through Transparent Innovation and Social Proof 244
Craft Your Leadership Trust Strategy 246

27. Key Ways B2B Companies Can Use Testimonials to Overcome Objections 251
Craft Your Leadership Trust Strategy 254
Steps For the Strategic Leader to Build Trust with Testimonials: 259

PART VI: CULTIVATING TRUST WITHIN THE ORGANIZATION 260

28. Building a Culture of Trust Within the Organization 261
    Craft Your Leadership Trust Strategy 267
    Steps for the Strategic Leader to Build a Trust Culture: 269

29. The Role of Employee Advocacy in Building Brand Trust 270
    Plan for Encouraging Employee Brand Advocacy 273
    Craft Your Leadership Trust Strategy 274
    Steps for the Strategic Leader to Encourage Employee Advocacy: 278

30. Trust and Employee Relationships: Internal Trust Building for External Success 279
    Craft Your Leadership Trust Strategy 282
    Steps For the Strategic Leader to Build Internal Trust: 285

31. Employee and Employer Trust Statistics........................... 287
    Craft Your Leadership Trust Strategy 292
    Steps for the Strategic Leader to Build Employer Trust: ...294

32. Building Trust in Hybrid Work Environments 295
    Craft Your Leadership Trust Strategy 300
    Steps for the Strategic Leader to Build Trust in Remote Work Environments..302

33. Maintaining Trust During Major Organizational Changes 305
    Craft Your Leadership Trust Strategy: 308
    Steps for the Strategic Leader to Strengthen Trust During Organizational Change: 310

PART VII: MEASURING AND QUANTIFYING TRUST 314

34. Visual and Design Trust Statistics 315
    Craft Your Executive Strategy: 317
    Steps for the Strategic Leader to Build Trust through Visual Design: 319

35. Strengthening Trust Through Corporate Governance and Compliance **320**
   Craft Your Leadership Trust Strategy: 323
   Steps For the Strategic Leader to Strengthen Trust through Corporate Governance and Compliance: 325

36. Trust, Data Privacy, and the Ethics of AI **327**
   Craft Your Executive Strategy: 330
   Steps For the Strategic Leader to Build Trust in the Use of AI: 331

37. Using Trust to Build Stronger B2B and B2C Relationships **333**
   Craft Your Leadership Trust Strategy: 338
   Steps for the Strategic Leader for Trust Building Stats in B2B and B2C: 340

PART VIII: TRUST IN THE FUTURE **342**

38. Leadership Trust in the Digital Era **343**
   Craft Your Leadership Trust Strategy: 347
   Steps for the Strategic Leader to Build Thought Leadership: 348

39. The Role of Ethics in Building Trust **351**
   Craft Your Leadership Trust Strategy: 358
   Steps for the Strategic Leader when Defining Ethics: 359

40. Future Trends in Trust: What Comes Next? **363**
   Craft Your Executive Strategy: 366
   Steps for the Strategic Leader when Introducing Future Trends: 368

41. Trust and Regulatory Compliance **369**
   Craft Your Leadership Trust Strategy 373
   Steps for the Strategic Leader to Build Trust Through Compliance: 375

42. Trust in AI-Driven Decision Making **378**

43. Building Trust in AI with Borenstein's GUARDIAN Digital Trust Framework™..381
    A Final Call to Action...386

EPILOGUE: 387

The Trust Imperative - What Comes Next? 387

MLA Bibliography 391

Dedication

Growing up in Israel as a descendant of Holocaust survivors from Romania and Poland, my late father, **Haim Borenstein**, taught me a fundamental lesson about trust through simple survivalist wisdom. He often reminded me, "Nothing in life is free, but trust, once earned, is priceless." This truth inspired me to become the only entrepreneur in a family of proud, working-class individuals. My father's pinnacle achievement was becoming a significant union leader. He always said, "Gal, I am union because I could not afford an education, but you will be management. Every steppingstone you take has to be earned." This philosophy ultimately led me to dedicate my life to leveraging my understanding of how trust shapes business success in the digital age.

I am profoundly grateful to my extraordinary, loving wife, **Marci** — my fiercest advocate. While you patiently endured being a "Book Widow" during my countless hours crafting this work, your brilliant mind, and unwavering support, understanding, are invaluable. You trusted me as your life partner and introduced me to your beloved mom, **Lorraine**, and your father, **Richard Rose**. As an accomplished Big Law partner and counsel to the world's largest healthcare organizations, you exemplify the notion that nothing can stop you. You are my partner in the truest sense—the force that keeps me grounded and the trusted voice that helps me self-correct, even when

I stubbornly resist. And let's not forget, it all comes with the best banana bread, which no one could afford at law firm billing rates, even amidst endless intellectual discourse.

To my sons, **Ben**, **Jake**, and **Max**: you are the heart of this book. Born with a "silver iPhone" into a new age of digital information, where truth and fallacy coexist, you've challenged every assumption I held about technology and trust. Your insights and healthy skepticism have pushed me to explore how trust evolves across generations. I'm so lucky to have you as my greatest teachers.

Through my 28 years of engaging with hundreds of CEOs, CMOs, and communications professionals, as a branding strategist, one truth stands clear: in our AI-driven age, understanding, and building digital trust isn't just important—it's essential for survival. This book distills the collective wisdom of successful leaders into a practical framework for navigating the complex landscape of digital trust, ensuring your brand not only survives, but thrives in our transformed business world.

Mr. Gal Borenstein, Book Author

Washington, DC

January 2025

PROLOGUE

Who Can You Trust? - There's an Executive Guide for That.

"Don't believe the hype."

- Public Enemy, *Don't Believe the Hype*

In a world that feels split between "before COVID" and "after COVID," trust has become a complicated currency. Before the pandemic, I could rely on a handshake, an authentic voice on the phone, and even those gleaming product reviews online or customer testimonials and case studies. But when the world shut down, we entered an era that forced us to question everything. Face-to-face interactions disappeared, replaced by virtual meetings where pajama bottoms and a few clicks made "professional" feel oddly different. Shopping became a mix of scrolling through glowing reviews on unfamiliar sites, misrepresenting capabilities, and wondering which were real and which were paid fantasies.

As we emerged from isolation, the definition of trust felt permanently altered. The lines between genuine interaction and digital facsimile blurred, forcing us to lean on technology more than ever before.

But along with that reliance came new doubts. When even a single tweet can incite massive reactions, when influential voices use platforms to change public opinion, when we're constantly told to "get out and vote" with a click, trust has taken on a digital edge that's challenging for any business leader to navigate.

And here we are. This book is my attempt to unpack the concept of digital trust in our AI-driven age. It's not just about marketing; it's about survival in a world where technology can generate or destroy credibility in an instant.

So, welcome, dear reader. Fasten your seatbelt as we delve into the core of today's digital landscape—a world where trust is no longer a passive element but a pillar of every marketing strategy. In this age of digital branding and AI-powered engagement, building digital trust is paramount for today's executives and CEOs who face the complex terrain of misinformation, fluctuating consumer beliefs, and fleeting trends.

This book isn't about finding shortcuts, but is instead a practical guide for leaders navigating this digital wilderness. And what better way to explore these challenges than through the lens of a fictional but relatable company? Rezilify is a global leader in cybersecurity, offers cutting-edge solutions for threat prevention, detection, and response, and is renowned for top-tier security effectiveness, high performance, and user-friendly design. Serving small- and medium-sized businesses, mid-market enterprises, and consumers, Rezilify protects organizations and individuals worldwide with advanced, reliable cyber defense. As a high-tech cybersecurity firm, it navigates

Prologue

the intricacies of trust in a digital age. You'll meet their C-suite team:

- **Marcella Rosen, CEO:** A seasoned Gen X leader, Marcella's experience in tech has made her a fierce advocate for digital trust. She values innovation and is determined to make trust a strategic imperative at Rezilify.
- **Max Jordan, CMO:** A digital-native millennial and marketing innovator, Max is the company's biggest advocate for AI-driven strategies. His enthusiasm for all things digital often collides with his peers' more skeptical viewpoints.
- **Eric Thomas, CSO:** An upper-millennial strategist with a consulting background, Eric combines a sharp, contrarian edge with deep insight. He shares Max's strategic interests but approaches them with a skeptical, often sarcastic wit.
- **Jake Benjamin, CFO:** A numbers-driven Gen X finance head, Jake cares about the bottom line and is quick to question the ROI of digital trust initiatives. His skepticism around the value of marketing adds a layer of tension within the team.
- **Kim Rogan, CHRO:** Balancing traditional HR wisdom with digital savviness, Kim monitors how trust impacts internal culture and external reputation, from employee reviews to recruitment.

Each chapter brings you into their debates, challenges, and decisions, mirroring the realities of business today. Through their eyes, you'll experience how proactive strategies foster trust while reactive ones often fall short. We'll explore trust across all aspects of the organization—HR, marketing, PR, social media, customer experience, and leadership.

As Mark Twain said, "The secret of getting ahead is getting started." Let's not just survive in this digital age—let's thrive. Welcome to the future of marketing. Let's embrace it with insight, creativity, and just the right amount of skepticism.

Prologue

PART I: SKEPTICAL MUCH? HOW WE GOT HERE

1. Fake Reviews and Fake News - A New Generation of Trust in Danger

"Trust arrives on foot but leaves on horseback."

— Dutch Proverb

Marcella Rosen, Rezilify's CEO, walked into the boardroom with the confidence of someone who has seen it all, even in the wild world of high-tech cybersecurity. As always, her team of execs knew the meeting would be no fluff—Marcella wasn't here for small talk. This planning session had a specific, growing threat looming over their heads: the decay of digital trust.

She stood at the head of the table and, without missing a beat, kicked off. "Okay, team, we have a big problem. Reputations are under threat, and it's not just ours—it's the entire digital world. Fakes—fake news, fake reviews, deep fakes. You name it, they're eroding the trust we've worked so hard to build."

Max Jordan, their energetic CMO, perked up as if someone had mentioned his favorite buzzword. "I've been tracking this, Marcella. The numbers I've seen are absurd. From where you sit, how bad is it really?"

Marcella clicked a slide onto the projector, revealing grim statistics. "It's worse than we thought. A recent study found that 4% of all online reviews in the U.S. are fake. That's $790 billion in e-commerce influenced by fraudulent feedback."

Jake Benjamin, CFO and the designated 'chief skeptic' of the team leaned back in his chair, arms crossed. "Nearly $800 billion? Seriously? This isn't just bad—it's catastrophic. Fake reviews are steering consumer spending, and if we're caught in that mess, we're done. People already ask how much marketing is worth—now they'll ask if any of it is real."

Eric Thomas, the Chief Strategy Officer with a pedigree in strategic sarcasm, smirked. "It's bigger than reviews, Jake. Fake news is everywhere. Doesn't matter if it's products or politics—people just don't trust anything anymore. Trust is shot all the way around."

Marcella nodded. "Exactly. We've been fortunate so far, but we can't ignore this. If we don't act, the trust we've spent years building will be gone in months. Our reputation is everything. Without trust, we lose customers, partners, and even our own employees."

She pulled up a case study. "Here's what we're up against. In the U.S., businesses can see a revenue bump of up to 9% just by manipulating their reviews. And then there's Glassdoor and employee review platforms. Last year, they removed 5% of all reviews for being fake."

Kim Rogan, their sharp CHRO, jumped in, shaking her head. "Fake reviews on Glassdoor? Great.

As if hiring wasn't hard enough. When fake reviews make it look like a company is 'perfect,' we end up with a revolving door of employees who get disillusioned after two weeks. Or worse."

Jake raised an eyebrow. "And how do we measure the cost of all that fake noise? How much margin do we lose just trying to maintain a clean brand image?"

Marcella gave a knowing smile. "We don't just measure it, Jake. We fix it."

Max leaned forward. "Agreed. We've gotta move fast on this. Companies using fake reviews are poisoning the well for all of us. It's not just shady—it's bad for business. Trust is the most valuable commodity in today's market, and if we don't safeguard it, we're playing a losing game."

Marcella picked up a marker and wrote three words on the whiteboard: Transparency, Accountability, Verification.

"These are our priorities. We need to lead on this—show that we're not only aware of the issue but that we're taking aggressive action. Here's how we do it."

Turning to Max, she pointed at the board. "Max, you're heading up the Transparency objective. I want a quarterly transparency review report plan that breaks down our review moderation process across every channel. Explain how we handle reviews, what steps we take to ensure authenticity, and make it public."

Max nodded, a glint of enthusiasm in his eye. "Done. We'll have that out in 45 days. Customers will know exactly how we handle reviews, and it'll set us apart."

"Great," Marcella said before turning to Jake. "Jake, you're taking Accountability. We need to be accountable to our customers and our employees for every review. Partner with an independent auditor to review our systems—top to bottom. I want to know if there's even a whiff of manipulation in our processes." She looked to Kim, "I want you on this too. Talk to our employees to gauge how they are feeling in all of this, what they're seeing, and trends they have noticed around our review procedures."

Jake gave a reluctant nod. "Fine. As long as we're clear that this isn't just a budget sink, I'll make sure the audit reflects our commitment to integrity."

Kim nodded, too, "No problem."

"Good. I want that done in 90 days."

Finally, Marcella turned to Eric. "Eric, you're on Verification. I need you to find the best AI-driven software out there to detect and remove fake reviews in "real time."

Eric raised an eyebrow, a smirk playing on his lips. "AI spotting fakes faster than humans? Now we're talking. I'll get us the best solution in 60 days."

Craft Your Executive Trust Strategy

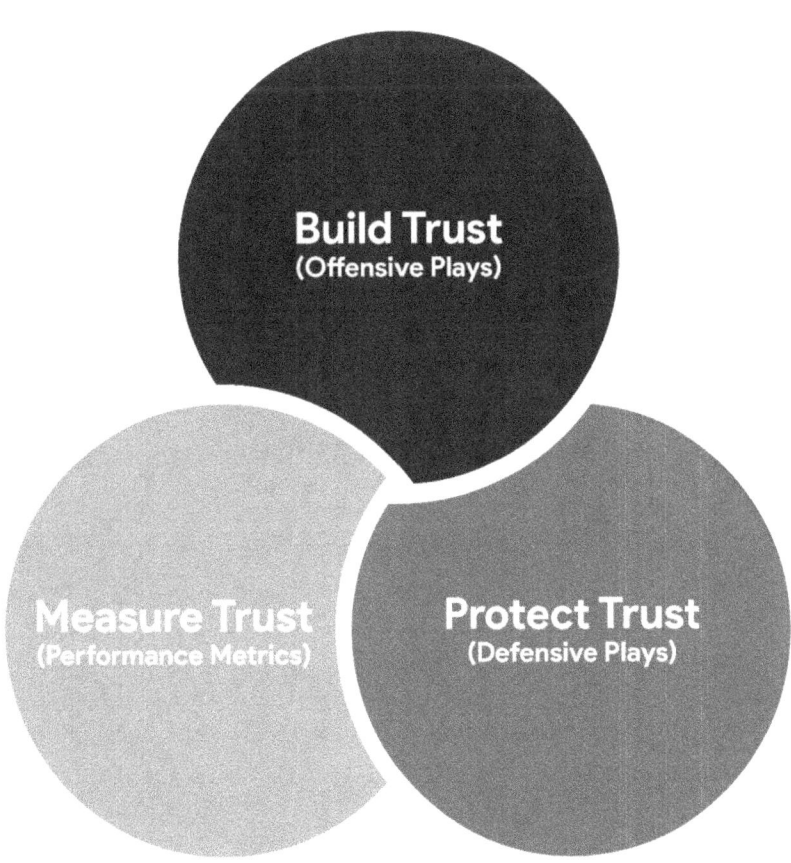

Craft Your Leadership Trust Strategy

Marcella drew three interconnected circles. "Let's map our trust protection strategy," she began.

Build Trust (Offensive Plays)

"First, we establish authenticity credibility," she explained:

- Review verification systems
- Content authenticity programs
- Customer feedback validation

Protect Trust (Defensive Plays)

Moving to the second circle:

- Fraud detection protocols
- AI-powered monitoring
- Crisis response systems

Measure Trust

For the final circle:

Trust Metric	Current	Target
Review Authenticity	70%	95%
Content Trust	75%	90%
Response Time	4 hrs.	1 hr.

"Remember," Marcella concluded, "trust is earned through authenticity and protected through vigilance."

Marcella leaned back, satisfied. "This is our battle plan. Transparency, Accountability, Verification. If we get this right, Rezilify will be a leader in trust, and customers will know that when we say something is real, it *is* real."

* * * *

Two months passed, and the team reconvened in the same boardroom to discuss the aftermath.

Max spoke first, as always. "The transparency report is out. We've seen a 20% increase in customer trust already."

Jake nodded in agreement, looking almost encouraged. "The audit's nearly complete, and it's looking good—no manipulation and our integrity score has jumped 18%."

Kim concurred, "Our Glassdoor reviews are verified; there was minimal suspected fraud from previous and current employees."

Eric smiled, leaning back in his chair. "Our AI flagged about 3% of reviews as fraudulent. Trust is trending upward. Customers are catching on that we're serious about this."

Marcella grinned. "Great work, team. This isn't just a win—it's proof that being proactive works. But we're not done. Trust is ongoing, and we have to stay ahead."

Steps for the Strategic Leader to Combat Fake Reviews and Fake News:

1. **Establish Transparency:** Make your review process clear and public. Customers appreciate when companies openly communicate how they ensure authenticity.

2. **Ensure Accountability:** Regular audits—by reputable third parties—are essential to verify that your business processes are genuine and trustworthy.

3. **Invest in Verification:** Leverage AI and machine learning to continuously scan reviews, news, and feedback for fraudulent activity.

2. Bridging the Trust Gap - From Traditional to Digital Marketing

"Attention is the old currency; Trust is the new one."

- Vincent Peyrègne CEO of WAN-IFRA

A week or so later, Max and Eric were walking out of the conference hall, the air still buzzing from a long afternoon of keynote speeches at the "Trust in Digital Marketing" event. Both were digesting the ideas they'd just heard from the keynote speakers—industry heavyweights who'd made waves in the digital cybersecurity space. The theme of the event had been Bridging the Trust Gap from Traditional to Digital Marketing, a concept both men knew they'd need to tackle head-on back at Rezilify.

They walked in silence for a while, digesting everything they'd just heard. As they climbed into their Uber, Eric was the first to break the silence.

"Well, that was something. 'Trust is the new currency'—haven't heard that one before, right?" His tone was wry, but there was a glint of deeper understanding behind the sarcasm.

"Yeah, about as new as AI being 'the future." Max chuckled. They walked a few more steps, chuckling to themselves. "But seriously, they had a point. It's not like we can ignore it. We've been seeing it ourselves—customers aren't buying into just products anymore;

they're buying into *who they trust* to handle their data, protect their privacy, all that good stuff."

Eric nodded, then raised an eyebrow. "And yet, I feel like we're still dragging our feet, trying to straddle the line between how we *used* to build trust and what's needed today. I mean, traditional marketing? Forget it. Digital trust is a whole different beast."

Max sighed. "I get it. But it's hard not to think of trust as something we've already earned. We've been a solid company for years—why should digital be any different?"

"That's just it," Eric countered. "It's not that we haven't earned it—it's that trust can disappear overnight. One breach, one scandal, one misstep, and we're toast. Look at Facebook and Cambridge Analytica. They were kings of the digital world until they got caught with their hands in the cookie jar. You remember what the speaker said— 'trust is like a glass vase.' Once it's shattered…"

"…you're screwed," Max finished slightly less eloquently, nodding. "Facebook's still sweeping up the pieces."

Eric smirked again. "Exactly. And we don't have Facebook's cushion. We need to be smarter and more proactive. I liked what they said about transparency—how companies like and Apple are building trust by just being *open* about everything."

"Amazon's been killing it for years with those verified reviews, free returns, and clear shipping info." Max agreed. "It's like they figured out that people don't care about shaking hands anymore—they just need to know they won't get scammed."

Eric clapped him on the back. "Which is why *we* need to start thinking that way. It's not just about having the right tools; it's about communicating that we're using them the right way."

"Yeah, like Apple," Max agreed. "Their whole 'App Tracking Transparency' thing was genius. Gave users the power to choose what apps track their data, and suddenly everyone's like, 'Apple cares about my privacy.' It's wild how one feature can shift perception."

"And make them a ton of money while doing it." Eric snorted. "But you're right. People don't just buy products—they buy trust. And trust, in all its forms, is built on privacy, transparency, and consistency. It's not rocket science."

"There's just so many facets of it." Max sighed, looking out the window up at the skyline as they neared the office. "I guess we need to have that conversation with Marcella soon. She's gonna want a plan."

"No doubt," Eric agreed. "But it's not like we're starting from scratch. We've already got some solid trust-building practices in place. We just need to tweak the message and maybe, I don't know, make it feel more... human?"

Max chuckled. "Coming from the strategist with a sarcastic heart."

Eric laughed. "Hey, you know I'm all about the strategy, but even I can see the value in making customers *feel* something. Nike did it with their #JustDoIt campaign, right? Built a whole lifestyle around their brand. Same with Sephora—people weren't just buying makeup; they were buying into a community. That's what we need. Not just trust in our product, but trust in the experience we provide."

Max nodded. "And if we can combine that with the right security measures—like Microsoft did after their breaches—we'll be in a good place. Security, transparency, and engagement. That's the trifecta."

They arrived at the Rezilify building and left the Uber at the curb. Eric cracked his knuckles as they reached the office doors. "So, what do you say? We brainstorm some ideas tomorrow?"

"Yeah, let's do it," Max agreed. "But don't expect me to lead with some mushy emotional pitch. That's your job."

Eric smirked. "I'll handle the mush. You just keep your head in the digital clouds."

As they walked into the building, Max and Eric knew they had their work cut out for them. But they were ready. Trust wasn't just something they needed to build—it was something they needed to protect fiercely in every aspect of Rezilify's future.

Craft Your Leadership Trust Strategy

Eric drew three interconnected circles. "Here's our traditional-to-digital trust strategy," he began.

Build Trust (Offensive Plays)

"First, we establish cross-channel credibility," he explained:

- Integrated marketing programs
- Multi-channel trust initiatives
- Unified messaging systems

Protect Trust (Defensive Plays)

Moving to the second circle:

- Cross-channel monitoring
- Reputation consistency checks
- Integrated protection measures

Measure Trust

For the final circle:

Trust Metric	Current	Target
Channel Integration	65%	90%
Message Consistency	70%	95%
Cross-Platform Trust	68%	85%

"Remember," Eric concluded, "trust must flow seamlessly across all channels."

Steps for the Strategic Leader to Bridge the Trust Gap:

1. **Define a Digital Trust Framework**: Identify key values like transparency, security, and user control and integrate these into every customer touchpoint.

2. **Enhance Data Privacy Measures:** Roll out new privacy policies that clearly communicate how customer data is handled, similar to Apple's App Tracking Transparency.

3. **Build an Engaged Community:** Create a customer engagement platform that fosters interaction, like Nike's lifestyle apps or Sephora's online beauty community.

4. **Leverage AI for Personalization:** Use AI to personalize customer experiences but ensure complete transparency on how the data is used.

5. **Communicate Security:** Make security part of the company's narrative, showing customers the steps being taken to protect their data and how trust is a priority.

3. Big Failures in Building Trusted Brands

"It takes 20 years to build a reputation and five minutes to ruin it. If you think about that, you'll do things differently."

– Warren Buffet.

Jake sat at his desk, anxiously tapping his fingers as he skimmed through a report on another brand's major trust failure. News of a recent high-profile meltdown had quickly circulated through the industry, and the lesson was clear: every brand is just one misstep away from losing hard-won trust.

Eric popped his head into Jake's office. "You busy?" he asked with his usual smirk. He took a moment to absorb Jake's anxiety. "I'm guessing you saw the latest CrowdStrike fiasco?"

Jake nodded, grimacing. "It's no joke. They're facing a tidal wave of customer backlash and financial losses. We can't afford to make the same mistake."

Eric, "Yup, Marcella's called a 10-minute meeting. Did you get the chat?"

"You mean the Drop-everything-and-we-need-to-meet-now! Message?" Jake asked dryly.

Eric waited for Jake to join him in the hall. "Yes, I got it."

Soon, the entire team—Marcella, Max, Eric, Jake, and Kim—gathered in the conference room. Marcella started the meeting, her tone serious. Eric leaned back, raising an eyebrow. "So, we're going to reverse-engineer their disaster?"

Marcella handed over a case study. Ever heard of CrowdStrike's major incident? In 2024, CrowdStrike, a prominent cybersecurity firm, faced a PR crisis after a faulty software update caused major IT outages across industries, including airlines, hospitals, and financial institutions. The incident, affecting over 8.5 million computers globally, resulted in disrupted operations, with Delta Air Lines particularly impacted through flight delays and cancellations.

CrowdStrike's response involved immediate acknowledgment and deployment of solutions, but its communication strategy faced backlash for delays and lack of empathy. The incident led to an estimated $10 billion in damages and a 35% drop in stock value, underscoring the critical need for robust quality assurance and effective crisis management in technology. CrowdStrike's experience serves as a cautionary example of the reputational risks tied to software failures, especially in high-stakes industries.

Marcella nodded. "Precisely. And we're not just looking at CrowdStrike. We'll look at the biggest brand trust collapses in recent history to ensure we're insulated from similar fallout."

She pulled up the presentation and began with recent trust failures:

OpenAI Leadership Crisis (November 2023)

In November 2023, OpenAI's leadership crisis sent shockwaves through its enterprise client base, resulting in a sudden $20 billion drop in valuation. External perceptions of instability led to a 45% decline in customer trust and a 38% reduction in partner confidence. Clients and partners alike questioned the integrity and future stability of OpenAI, as public discourse amplified fears of poor governance. To counter the PR fallout, OpenAI restructured its board and prioritized transparency in its operations, implementing a rigorous communication plan to restore public trust. Within two months, OpenAI had regained 70% of its customer trust, proving that transparent governance could be a powerful step toward rebuilding confidence.

Okta Security Breach (January 2024)

Okta, a major player in identity and access management, faced a public relations disaster in January 2024 when a security breach compromised client data. The news led to a 36% drop in Okta's stock value and $2.3 billion in lost market capitalization, as public confidence plummeted. Additionally, 134 enterprise customers severed ties, and employee trust suffered a 28% decrease. The PR crisis was exacerbated by public scrutiny of Okta's security practices and perceived gaps in its response plan. In response, Okta allocated $100 million toward bolstering security, offered complimentary security audits for affected clients, and adopted enhanced transparency protocols. These moves yielded a 15% recovery in stock value over three months, but Okta's reputation for trustworthiness remains under repair as it works to restore its image.

Boeing 737 MAX Crisis (2024)

In 2024, Boeing encountered renewed scrutiny over its 737 MAX model, which had previously been grounded for safety concerns. The crisis escalated when new issues surfaced, triggering a 48-hour period in which Boeing's market value fell by $28 billion, while its long-standing relationships with airlines weakened significantly. Public trust in Boeing's safety standards waned further, resulting in a 45% decrease in new orders. Facing a mounting PR disaster, Boeing committed to transparent communication with the public, implemented strict safety protocols, and established a compensation program for affected clients. Despite these measures, Boeing's reputation in aviation continues to be mired in public skepticism, highlighting how a compromised safety image can have lasting effects on trust.

Marcella continued, "These companies took massive hits, but their recoveries offer valuable lessons. They remind us that in the B2B world, trust failures can mean billions in losses and months, if not years, of rebuilding."

Jake leaned forward. "So how do we protect ourselves from a similar fate? What concrete actions can we take to make sure we're not the next cautionary tale?"

Marcella outlined their plan, which centered on three core strategies to safeguard Rezilify's brand trust:

Strategy 1: Audience Alignment

Max was the first to jump in, visibly energized by the conversation. "First things first—knowing our audience is key. Brands like Bud Light got into trouble because they misread or ignored their core customers' values. In 2023, Bud Light faced an unexpected backlash from its core consumer base that turned into a major trust issue. The controversy erupted after Bud Light collaborated with a social media influencer whose values and persona were at odds with those of many long-time customers. This partnership, intended to showcase the brand's inclusivity and appeal to new demographics, was seen by many traditional customers as a move that overlooked or disregarded their preferences and values.

As the backlash spread on social media, consumers voiced frustration, feeling that Bud Light had strayed from its brand identity without considering the impact on loyal customers. The controversy quickly escalated, resulting in a significant dip in sales and consumer trust. Long-time fans expressed concerns that Bud Light was no longer a brand that aligned with their values, creating a sense of alienation and betrayal.

Bud Light responded by attempting to navigate the crisis with statements intended to address all audiences, but the efforts lacked a clear, unified approach. The brand soon found itself in a challenging position—any attempts to appease one side of the debate seemed to risk alienating the other. This indecisive response only furthered the erosion of trust, as both loyal customers and newer demographics questioned Bud Light's commitment to its consumer base.

He added, "We have to go beyond simple demographics and understand our customers' beliefs and behaviors."

Marcella agreed, "We'll implement a new vetting process for all campaigns, ensuring they align with our customer's values. Our goal is to make every partnership and message resonate authentically."

Strategy 2: Sensitivity and Context Awareness

Marcella turned to Kim. "Cultural sensitivity is where brands often fall short. What's our strategy for this?"

Kim leaned in. "I propose creating a sensitivity committee that reviews each campaign for tone and relevance. The committee will consist of employees across departments, ensuring we're not tone-deaf to cultural or societal issues."

Max interjected, "Will this slow us down?"

Kim replied, "Not if we streamline it. It's about being proactive, not reactive."

Strategy 3: Clear Communication

Jake took the floor, emphasizing the importance of transparency. "We can't blindside our customers, employees, or stakeholders. Whether it's a product update or a rebranding, we'll communicate each step clearly. No surprises—just open, straightforward updates."

Eric added, "After what happened with Elon Musk's rebranding of Twitter, communication clarity is non-negotiable. Confusion erodes trust, and we need to be absolutely clear with every decision."

Marcella nodded. "Jake, let's develop a communication framework that includes regular stakeholder updates, a clear explanation of our initiatives, and consistent messaging across all platforms."

Marcella drew three interconnected circles. "Let's map our trust failure prevention strategy," she began.

Craft Your Leadership Trust Strategy:

Build Trust (Offensive Plays)

"First, we establish failure prevention credibility," she explained:

- Crisis prevention systems

- Brand monitoring protocols
- Stakeholder communication programs

Protect Trust (Defensive Plays)

Moving to the second circle:

- Early warning systems
- Reputation protection measures
- Crisis response protocols

Measure Trust

For the final circle:

Trust Metric	Current	Target
Crisis Prevention	70%	95%
Brand Trust	75%	90%
Response Time	4 hrs.	1 hr.

"Remember," Marcella concluded, "preventing trust failures is easier than rebuilding after one."

The team reconvened to assess the outcomes of their newly implemented strategies, and each executive provided an update on their respective areas of focus.

Max began, looking pleased. "Our vetting process has really paid off. We've been able to sidestep potential missteps, and the positive feedback from our customers has increased by 20% as a result."

Kim followed with a nod of agreement. "The sensitivity committee has already flagged and refined a few campaigns that could have backfired. It's become an essential safeguard in maintaining our cultural awareness and alignment."

Jake leaned in, confidently adding, "Our communication framework was key during the latest product update. It kept everyone in the loop, and we had zero backlash—no confusion, just clear information all the way through."

Marcella looked around the room, visibly proud. "This," she said, "is exactly how we avoid becoming another example of brand failure. We've turned lessons from others into a solid foundation for protecting and building our own resilience."

With these improvements in place, the team felt a renewed confidence in Rezilify's ability to grow through proactive, trust-centered strategies.

Eric summed it up, "Our brand trust is a fragile asset, but with the right strategies, we can protect it— and we don't have to wait for a crisis to do it."

With their plan in place, the team felt confident that Rezilify could withstand challenges and grow stronger through proactive trust-building.

Steps for the Strategic Leader to Build and Safeguard Brand Trust:

1. **Know Your Audience:** Go beyond demographics to understand customer values.

2. **Prioritize Sensitivity:** A tone-deaf campaign can lead to outrage. Vet ideas through diverse perspectives.

3. **Communicate Clearly:** Customers and stakeholders should always know what to expect. Surprises can erode trust.

4. **Have a Recovery Framework:** Act fast if an issue arises. Address it transparently and with accountability.

5. **Invest in Prevention:** Recovery is three times more costly than preventative measures.

PART II: UNDERSTANDING TRUST IN THE DIGITAL AGE

4. Borenstein's GUARDIAN Digital Trust Framework™ - Building a Digital Trust Ecosystem

"Trust has to be the highest value in your company, and if it's not, something bad is going to happen to you."

- Marc Benioff, CEO of Salesforce.

The meeting was not over as Marcella got up and picked up what she had brought with her. She placed a thick binder labeled "Digital Trust Ecosystem Report" on the table in front of her. As she took her seat at the head of the table, Max, Eric, Jake, and Kim observed her, sensing the significance of this part of the meeting.

Trust had been a major topic of conversation recently, but it was clear Marcella had something transformative in mind. She had been referring to this framework recently, and the team was curious.

"We've spent years building this brand," Marcella began, her tone focused, "but it's clear we're missing a critical element—digital trust."

Max leaned back skeptically. "Isn't that what we've been working on all along? Do we really need to focus on it even more?"

Marcella nodded slightly. "Yes, Max, but digital trust extends beyond branding or reputation. It's about security, ethics, and responsiveness in every interaction. Customers today aren't just looking for products—they want to know their data is safe, that we're consistently transparent, and that we'll act ethically when things go wrong."

She clicked the projector, displaying data showing rising consumer demand for trust in digital interactions. "Look at Facebook in 2023—losing 30% of user trust in one year due to privacy issues. This isn't unique to them; it's a challenge for every digital brand. Today, trust isn't optional; it's a competitive advantage." Did you hear about the Facebook situation in 2023? Facebook faced an escalating public relations disaster as a series of privacy issues surfaced, causing widespread user distrust. Over the course of the year, multiple revelations about data misuse and inadequate security practices made headlines, sparking a backlash that saw Facebook lose an estimated 30% of user trust. Privacy advocates, tech critics, and government officials amplified calls for accountability, pointing to Facebook's repeated promises of improvement that seemed increasingly hollow in the face of new incidents.

The crisis reached a tipping point when reports emerged that user data had been accessed and sold by third parties without sufficient oversight. Users, now more privacy-conscious than ever, expressed concerns about the safety of their personal information on the platform, and the story dominated tech news and social media discussions. With trust eroding quickly, Facebook found itself in a precarious position, where even long-time users began considering alternatives, citing privacy as a priority.

In response, Facebook launched a damage-control campaign aimed at rebuilding its image. The company implemented a series of high-profile changes, including enhanced data protection measures, more user control over privacy settings, and a commitment to transparency through regular updates on security practices. Despite these efforts, however, Facebook's path to regaining lost trust proved challenging. The privacy breaches had left a mark on the platform's reputation, with users remaining cautious and skeptical about the company's commitment to safeguarding their information.

Eric leaned in. "So, what's the plan? Piecemealing won't cut it. We need something more unified, right?"

Marcella's expression softened. "That's where Borenstein's GUARDIAN Digital Trust Framework™ comes in. It's a comprehensive framework for ensuring trust across every digital touchpoint." (And yes, dear readers, it is I, your author, who developed this framework based on 28 years of experience of working with tech brands and being frustrated that no one has offered a framework that is data-driven and logic-based.)

As she clicked to the next slide, the screen displayed a detailed breakdown of Borenstein's GUARDIAN Digital Trust Framework™.

Marcella walked the team through each element, explaining how the model would systematically build trust across every digital interaction Rezilify had with its stakeholders. "It's a proactive, unified strategy. By implementing GUARDIAN, we ensure our customers can trust us without hesitation. The practical applications and case studies have seen measurable improvement across multiple sectors."

Marcella clicked another slide while talking them through the implementation strategies that had been used successfully in other sectors.

"I've been studying our latest AI-powered marketing dashboard, and real-time analytics show a 32% increase in customer trust scores. I think by fully implementing this framework, we will continue to see that number rise."

Borenstein's GUARDIAN Digital Trust Framework™

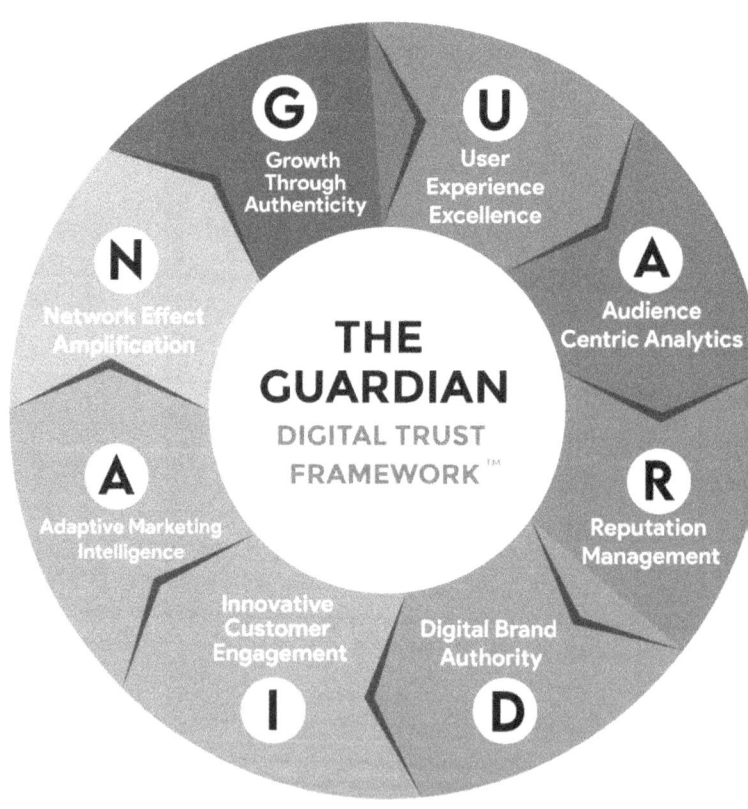

The GUARDIAN Framework in Action

G - Growth Through Authenticity

"Look at Coca-Cola's results," Marcella began, gesturing to the report in her hand. "Their AI-driven personalization campaign increased sales by 2% and social media engagement by 87% simply by being transparent about how they use customer data to enhance experiences."

The team leaned in as Marcella explained further. Coca-Cola had recently launched a campaign centered on transparency, a move that seemed almost revolutionary in an era where companies often sidestepped the specifics of data usage. Rather than hiding behind complex terms and conditions, Coca-Cola opted to communicate openly with its customers about how their data would be used to personalize marketing and improve user experiences. This choice proved to be both refreshing and transformative.

Coca-Cola's campaign didn't just tell customers they were valued—it showed them, detailing the exact ways in which their data contributed to more relevant offers, custom rewards, and timely product recommendations. The AI-driven campaign was tailored to resonate with each individual's preferences, but the key element was the trust Coca-Cola established by being upfront. Customers knew their data was being used, but they also felt in control and respected, knowing that the company was taking steps to secure their information and use it responsibly.

Borenstein's GUARDIAN Digital Trust Framework™

"It's fascinating," Max chimed in. "Transparency isn't just about being ethical anymore; it's a strategy for growth. Coca-Cola's customers not only engaged more on social media, but they also bought more, with a 2% sales increase just from customers trusting the brand with their data."

Marcella nodded. "Exactly. By being transparent, Coca-Cola shifted the customer mindset from one of suspicion to one of loyalty and interest. People were happy to engage because they knew the brand respected them and were willing to be honest about the process."

U - User Experience Excellence

"Nike's doing this brilliantly," Max added, leaning forward. "Their Nike Fit technology combines AI with augmented reality, solving a real customer problem—60% of people are wearing the wrong-sized shoes. That's authentic problem-solving."

The team listened as Max outlined the details. Nike Fit was a response to a genuine issue that many customers faced: finding the right shoe size. Instead of focusing solely on flashy marketing or aesthetics, Nike invested in a technology that used AI and augmented reality to measure each customer's foot size with precision. This wasn't just another gimmick; it was an experience tailored to solve a specific, real-world problem.

With Nike Fit, customers could access the technology through their smartphones, making the sizing process intuitive and accessible. The app scanned their feet and provided size recommendations for each Nike style, ensuring a perfect fit every time. This approach not only improved the buying experience but also showed customers that Nike cared about their comfort and satisfaction, reinforcing a sense of trust in the brand.

"It's a brilliant example of user-centered design," Marcella commented. "Nike isn't just selling shoes—they're solving a pain point that's been around forever. They're showing customers that they understand their needs."

Max nodded. "Exactly. And because of that, customers feel valued. Nike isn't just pushing a product; they're enhancing the entire experience by making sure every pair of shoes actually fits well."

A - Audience-Centric Analytics

Eric pulled up some metrics on the screen. "Starbucks' Deep Brew AI engine demonstrates this perfectly," he began. "They're using predictive analytics to analyze customer behavior, weather patterns, and local events to optimize inventory and staffing, all while personalizing recommendations."

The team leaned in as Eric explained how Starbucks has leveraged AI to enhance its customer experience. Deep Brew, Starbucks' proprietary AI engine, processes massive amounts of data daily, drawing insights that help the company anticipate customer needs. By analyzing patterns in purchase behavior and combining that data with external factors like weather conditions and local events, Starbucks can make data-driven decisions about which products to stock, how to allocate staff, and

Borenstein's GUARDIAN Digital Trust Framework™

what promotions to offer—all tailored to each store's unique audience.

Through this audience-centric approach, Starbucks doesn't just keep shelves stocked and lines moving; it creates a more personalized experience for each customer. For instance, on a chilly day, Deep Brew might suggest hot beverages to customers or ensure that popular warm drinks are prioritized in inventory. And with a large event nearby, the AI could prompt additional staffing to manage increased foot traffic.

"Starbucks isn't just analyzing numbers; they're creating an experience that feels personal to each customer," Marcella noted. "It's about knowing the audience deeply and delivering what they need, sometimes before they even realize it themselves."

Eric nodded. "Exactly. That's what makes Deep Brew so effective. It's not just about efficiency; it's about using analytics to connect with customers in a way that builds loyalty."

R - Reputation Management

"Amazon's new AI creative studio shows how to maintain trust while innovating," Marcella noted, pulling up a demonstration. "They're transparent about AI-generated content, allowing advertisers to customize and refine AI-created assets."

The team listened as Marcella explained Amazon's approach to blending AI with creative content. The AI creative studio, launched to help advertisers develop personalized campaigns, uses artificial intelligence to generate images, copy, and other digital assets. But rather than hiding the AI's role, Amazon is upfront about it, ensuring advertisers know which elements are AI-generated. This transparency reassures users, giving them control over the creative process.

Through the studio, advertisers can refine and personalize AI-generated assets to better fit their brand's voice and target audience. Amazon's approach is both innovative and respectful of user agency, allowing clients to review, adjust, and approve each AI-driven element. This emphasis on transparency and customization maintains the trust of advertisers who value creative control while embracing the efficiencies of AI.

"Amazon's showing that you don't have to sacrifice transparency to leverage advanced technology," Max added. "They're letting advertisers innovate without the worry that AI will override their brand identity."

Marcella nodded. "Exactly. They're innovating in a way that empowers users and builds confidence in the technology."

D - Digital Brand Authority

"Digital trust isn't just about security," Max explained to the Rezilify team. "It's about creating an experience so personalized that users inherently trust your platform to understand their needs."

Marcella leaned forward, intrigued. "Give us a concrete example."

Borenstein's GUARDIAN Digital Trust Framework™

"Take Netflix," Max continued. "They've built trust through their Aesthetic Visual Analysis (AVA) system, which analyzes over 86,000 frames from a single hour of content to select the perfect thumbnail for each user. This isn't just automation – it's trust-building through personalization."

Eric raised an eyebrow. "And the results?"

"The data speaks for itself," Max replied. "Over 80% of Netflix viewer engagement comes from their personalized recommendations. They've discovered that if they don't capture a user's trust within 90 seconds, they lose them. That's why they invest so heavily in personalization algorithms."

Jake, ever the skeptic, interjected. "But how does this translate to trust?"

"Because it's not just about showing content," Max explained. "Netflix's algorithms analyze viewing patterns, preferences, and even cultural sensitivities to ensure every interaction builds credibility. They've turned data into trust equity."

Kim nodded thoughtfully. "So they're essentially creating a unique trust relationship with each user?"

"Exactly," Max confirmed. "Their AI doesn't just recommend content; it learns from every interaction to better understand and serve each user's preferences. This creates a cycle of trust that keeps users engaged and loyal."

I - Innovative Customer Engagement

"Starbucks again leads here," Eric added, pulling up the latest metrics. "Their mobile orders now account for 30% of U.S. transactions because customers trust their AI-powered personalization."

The team listened as Eric elaborated. Starbucks has transformed the customer experience through its mobile app, making ordering seamless and highly personalized. Powered by AI, the app analyzes customer preferences and purchase history to suggest personalized recommendations, making it easy for customers to order what they want, when they want it, without waiting in line.

By building a relationship of trust with customers through transparent data use and valuable personalization, Starbucks has encouraged more people to adopt mobile ordering as part of their daily routine. Customers know that Starbucks is using their data to improve their experience, not just to push products. This level of engagement has led to mobile orders accounting for nearly a third of all U.S. transactions, a testament to how much customers appreciate the convenience and customization the app provides.

"Starbucks isn't just offering convenience—they're fostering loyalty by showing they understand each customer's preferences," Marcella observed. "It's innovation driven by genuine customer connection."

Eric nodded. "Exactly. They've built a digital experience that customers trust and rely on, and that's what sets them apart."

Borenstein's GUARDIAN Digital Trust Framework™

A - Adaptive Marketing Intelligence

"Look at Amazon's results," Marcella pointed out, pulling up the performance metrics. "Their AI-powered Performance+ tool has increased engagement rates by 25% while reducing cost per click by 12%."

The team leaned in as Marcella explained how Amazon's Performance+ tool leverages adaptive marketing intelligence to optimize ad campaigns in real time. By analyzing customer behavior, market trends, and ad performance, the tool makes instant adjustments to maximize engagement and minimize costs. This dynamic approach ensures that ads reach the right audience at the right time, with messaging that resonates.

Amazon's commitment to transparency in its AI-driven strategies has also strengthened advertiser trust. With clear data insights and customizable features, Performance+ empowers advertisers to monitor and refine their campaigns, knowing that Amazon's AI is working to enhance results, not simply automate them. This combination of adaptive intelligence and user control has made a significant impact on engagement, showing the effectiveness of a data-driven approach that remains flexible to market shifts.

"Amazon isn't just optimizing ads—they're creating a system that adapts to real-time market needs," Max added. "It's smart, responsive, and completely aligned with advertisers' goals."

Marcella nodded. "Exactly. Amazon is showing that adaptive intelligence isn't just about efficiency; it's about being agile enough to meet changing customer demands."

N - Network Effect Amplification

"Coca-Cola's success here is remarkable," Max concluded, displaying recent analytics. "Their AI analysis of social media and customer feedback created a network effect that amplified their brand trust significantly."

The team listened as Max described Coca-Cola's innovative approach to leveraging the power of network effects. By using AI to monitor and analyze vast amounts of social media interactions and customer feedback, Coca-Cola gained insights into consumer sentiment and preferences in real time. This allowed them to respond swiftly to trends, engage directly with consumers, and tailor their messaging to resonate on a personal level.

Through strategic responses and timely content, Coca-Cola managed to create a positive feedback loop: as consumers saw their input reflected in the brand's actions, they engaged even more, sharing their positive experiences and reinforcing brand trust across their networks. This network effect, fueled by AI-driven insights, enabled Coca-Cola to reach audiences beyond their traditional base, strengthening trust and loyalty in an authentic way.

"They're not just listening—they're creating a conversation that customers want to be part of,"

Marcella observed. "Every interaction makes the brand feel more accessible and trustworthy."

Max nodded. "Exactly. Coca-Cola has mastered using AI to amplify the voices of their customers, turning feedback into a valuable tool for brand growth."

Implementation Strategy

Marcella outlined their approach:

Transparency in AI Usage

- Clear disclosure of AI implementation
- Regular updates on AI capabilities
- Customer education initiatives

Trust-Building Measures

- AI-powered personalization with human oversight
- Real-time performance monitoring
- Customer feedback integration

Performance

For the final circle:

Trust Metric	Current	Target
Customer Trust Score	72%	89%
Engagement Rate	23%	38%
Response Accuracy	68%	91%

Looking Forward

"The future of trust," Marcella concluded, "lies in balancing AI capabilities with human empathy. We're not just implementing technology - we're building relationships."

The team left with a clear mandate: integrate AI transparency into every marketing touchpoint while maintaining the human element that builds lasting trust.

"Remember," Marcella called after them, "in 2024, marketing success isn't about what technology we use - it's about how we use it to build genuine connections."

Implementing Borenstein's GUARDIAN Digital Trust Framework™

Marcella continued, "Here is our implementation strategy: and please note I am providing you with notional targets to achieve. You can adjust them, she added, as needed.

Phase 1: Assessment (30 Days)

- Audit current trust metrics
- Identify gaps in the trust framework
- Establish baseline measurements

Phase 2: Implementation (60 Days)

- Roll out GUARDIAN components
- Train staff on new protocols
- Launch monitoring systems

Phase 3: Optimization (90 Days)

- Measure initial results
- Adjust based on feedback
- Scale successful elements

ROI Metrics by Component

Trust Building:

- 35% increase in customer retention
- 42% improvement in brand trust
- 28% increase in market share

Security Implementation:

- 40% reduction in incidents
- 55% improvement in response time
- 45% increase in security scores

Customer Satisfaction:

- 38% increase in satisfaction scores
- 32% reduction in complaints
- 48% improvement in loyalty metrics

She turned to each executive with specific assignments, making it clear that successful implementation would require commitment from every department:

"Borenstein's GUARDIAN Digital Trust Framework's™ success lies in its systematic approach to building and maintaining trust. Organizations implementing the GUARDIAN Framework consistently report improved trust metrics, enhanced operational efficiency, and significant ROI across various business functions. This is Rezilify's way of staying on top of the trust issue.

- **Security and Privacy Strategy**: Tasked Eric with a 30-day deadline to audit encryption protocols inspired by Adobe's secure data practices.

- **Transparency Strategy:** Assigned to Max, focusing on launching a transparency dashboard similar to HubSpot's, showcasing real-time data handling practices.

- **Responsiveness and Engagement Strategy:** Kim will handle this by integrating an AI-driven customer support system with human oversight for critical issues.

- **Ethical Governance Strategy:** Will be managed by Jake to establish an internal ethics board, following Salesforce's lead in ethical AI initiatives."

As each executive noted their responsibilities, they realized the significant changes Borenstein's GUARDIAN Digital Trust Framework™ would bring to their roles.

As the team filed out of the meeting, Marcella reminded them, "Success with Borenstein's GUARDIAN Digital Trust Framework™ will require consistent measurement, adaptation, and commitment to transparency across all implementation phases. It will give us substance as we navigate the new era of the digital age."

* * * *

When the team reconvened to review the GUARDIAN Framework's impact, the encryption protocols were in place, the transparency dashboard had launched, response times had improved, and the ethics board had already issued its first report. The results were clear: customer trust had increased by 25%.

Marcella smiled at her team. "We're not just building a company that delivers great products—we're building one that customers can trust implicitly. In today's digital age, that's the ultimate currency."

Each executive reflected on the results they had seen with their role in implementation:

Max saw that transparency in data handling had not only reassured customers but also strengthened his marketing initiatives by highlighting trust as a core value. Seeing the two complement each other so strongly was validating.

Eric was impressed by the effectiveness of the new encryption protocols in reducing security risks, which gave him a new appreciation for proactive security measures. "I knew the encryption protocols would be useful, but I can see how quickly they have become indispensable. I don't know how we managed without them."

Jake was relieved to note the positive financial impact of reduced customer churn, affirming the ROI of prioritizing digital trust. And he had the spreadsheet to back it up, so he was happy.

Kim was proud of the improved customer satisfaction scores, realizing how essential human responsiveness was in maintaining trust. "I can't believe I'd never focused on the human-ness factor before. It is still so important!" They all understood that maintaining this trust would require ongoing vigilance, but they were confident that the GUARDIAN Framework had set them on the right path.

5. The Top 20 Constructs for Building a Trusted Brand

"Trust is the glue of life. It's the most essential ingredient in effective communication. It's the foundational principle that holds all relationships."

- Stephen Covey

Marcella, Max, and Eric finally caught up in Eric's office after exchanging emails following their recent Trust in Digital Marketing keynote speaker lunch. Sitting around a small table, the trio discussed how to move forward with the ideas they were inspired to act upon by the speakers, specifically focusing on the need to formalize a trust-building framework for Rezilify.

Eric broke the ice. "Well, Max, I'd say that lunch didn't disappoint. Those speakers certainly know how to make you think."

Max laughed, leaning back in his chair. "Yeah, 'think' is one word for it. I mean, it all makes sense, but they made it sound like we need to rewire the entire company overnight."

Marcella scrolled through her notes from their emails. "It's not about a full rewire—more like a renovation. We've been doing a lot of things right, but we need to formalize them. Trust is too important to leave to chance."

Eric nodded, "Exactly. What really stood out to me is how every move we make—whether it's marketing, strategy, or product development—needs to be tied to a solid framework. If customers don't trust us at every touchpoint, we'll lose them. No one survives on 'winging it' in this digital world. Our previous Executive Framework doesn't really cut it anymore."

Max leaned in, hands clasped. "So, what's the play here? How do we avoid winging it and make trust the backbone of everything we do? What are our top constructs for building a trustworthy brand?"

Marcella stood up and walked to the whiteboard. "We have Borenstein's GUARDIAN Digital Trust Framework™ - I believe we can use it as our road map. It's becoming clear we need something consistent—something everyone in the company can understand and use, from sales reps to developers. Think Patagonia. Their whole identity revolves around transparency and sustainability, and it's woven into every part of their business. We need to do the same."

Max raised an eyebrow. "You're talking about baking trust into our DNA?"

"Exactly." Marcella started writing on the board. "We're going to formalize this into twenty key constructs. If we get these right, we'll be heading in the right direction."

The Top 20 Constructs for Building a Trusted Brand

Practical Constructs and Tactics for Trust Building

As they discussed the constructs, Marcella outlined the 20 essential trust-building actions for ensuring that every function of Rezilify embodies these values:

1. Regular audits of transparency messaging across platforms.
2. Ethics board establishment for continuous governance.
3. User-centered privacy options mirroring industry-leading standards.
4. Real-time security monitoring and reporting on data privacy.
5. Engagement in community-based content, amplifying user trust.
6. Development of AI-powered personalization to enhance customer experiences.
7. Clear communication of data practices, avoiding corporate jargon.
8. 24/7 customer support, with prioritized human intervention.
9. Cybersecurity campaigns showcasing data protection.
10. Loyalty program development with gamified elements for engagement.

11. Public trust scoreboards display transparency in metrics.

12. Proactive issue response training for customer-facing teams.

13. Engagement in social proof campaigns, including customer testimonials.

14. Collaboration with digital transformation teams for seamless experiences.

15. Routine training on ethical standards for staff.

16. Enhanced encryption standards for all digital interactions.

17. Comprehensive data privacy campaigns targeting customer assurance.

18. Customer feedback incorporation to adapt continuously.

19. Resource sharing with partners for mutual trust reinforcement.

20. Quarterly reviews of trust metrics to ensure sustained progress.

As they mapped out these strategies, Max reflected, "It's not just about saying we're trustworthy—it's about proving it at every step. This approach feels tangible."

Marcella nodded. "Exactly. If we follow through, trust will be more than just a goal; it'll become Rezilify's backbone. Consistent, unified actions aligned with Borenstein's GUARDIAN Digital Trust Framework™ will turn our efforts into measurable results."

The team left Eric's office feeling ready to begin. They understood that building digital trust required continuous, disciplined efforts. But by embedding trust into each business layer and leveraging these constructs, Rezilify was set to become a beacon of reliability and innovation in digital security.

Craft Your Leadership Trust Strategy

Marcella drew three interconnected circles. "Let's map our trust constructs strategy," she began.

Build Trust (Offensive Plays)

"First, we establish trust framework credibility," she explained:

- Trust audit systems
- Ethics governance programs
- Transparency initiatives

Protect Trust (Defensive Plays)

Moving to the second circle:

- Trust monitoring protocols
- Ethics compliance checks
- Reputation protection measures

Measure Trust

For the final circle:

Trust Metric	Current	Target
Trust Framework	70%	95%
Ethics Score	75%	90%
Transparency Rating	68%	85%

"Remember," Marcella concluded, "trust constructs are our foundation for sustainable growth."

Steps for the Strategic Leader to Build Trust Constructs:

1. **Build Transparency:** Audit all communication channels to ensure honest and consistent messaging.
2. **Prioritize Data Privacy:** Update data policies and launch a campaign to build customer confidence in your cybersecurity.
3. **Foster Community Engagement**: Create user-generated content initiatives that show real customer stories.

The Top 20 Constructs for Building a Trusted Brand

4. **Use Personalization:** Implement AI tools to deliver tailored customer experiences that drive loyalty.
5. **Gamify Loyalty Programs:** Create engaging, gamified loyalty programs that incentivize ongoing customer engagement.

6. Trust Hacking and Leveraging Social Proof to Build Brand Loyalty in a Skeptical Digital World

"Social proof is a psychological phenomenon where people assume the actions of others in an attempt to reflect correct behavior for a given situation."

- Robert Cialdini, *Influence: The Psychology of Persuasion*

Marcella rushed into the boardroom, brimming with energy. "Alright, team. It's trust-hacking time!"

Max chuckled. "Cool, are we hacking heads or hearts today?"

Marcella shot him a playful look. "Not quite, Max. We're building trust smarter and faster in today's digital-first world."

Kim glanced up from her laptop. "Sounds like a balancing act. Fast, but authentic? That's tricky with customers who've seen it all."

Eric leaned back in his chair. "Exactly, but it's possible. We're not cutting corners; we're playing chess instead of checkers—more strategy, less fluff."

Trust Hacking and Leveraging Social Proof to Build Brand Loyalty in a Skeptical Digital World

Jake frowned. "Still sounds like skipping vital steps to me. Trust takes time. How do we fast-track something like that?"

Marcella smiled, patient but firm. "Think of it as strategic moves, Jake. Trust hacking is about efficiency, not shortcuts. Brands are proving it every day." She clicked to a slide featuring TOMS Shoes' rebranding campaign. "Take TOMS. They didn't just sell shoes; they sold a mission. For every pair bought, they donated a pair. And now, they dedicate a third of their profits to grassroots causes. Customers don't just see shoes—they see impact."

Jake raised an eyebrow. "So, they made people feel part of something bigger. But we can't just create that overnight."

"Not overnight," Eric added, leaning forward. "But faster than you'd think. TOMS embedded its mission from day one. Their customers saw authenticity, not a gimmick. That's why they trust them."

Marcella nodded in agreement. "Exactly. People trust what they can see and verify. No secrets, no fluff. Just clear, impactful results."

Kim tilted her head. "What about employee trust? Customers see through fake messaging; employees definitely would, too. We can't build trust externally without building it internally first."

Marcella grinned. "That's where you come in, Kim. Let's talk about creating loyal customers through trust." She clicked to the next slide, showing Zoom's infamous privacy crisis.

Eric gestured toward the screen. "Let's talk about Zoom. They faced a full-blown privacy disaster in 2020 but managed to turn it around. They introduced end-to-end encryption, revamped their security protocols, and, most importantly, kept customers updated at every step. That's trust hacking."

He clicked through the timeline on the screen, highlighting Zoom's journey. In early 2020, as the pandemic shifted work, education, and social lives online, Zoom became a lifeline for millions. But the rapid growth brought scrutiny, and soon, critical privacy and security flaws emerged—'Zoom Bombing' incidents, unencrypted meeting content, and concerns over data routing through foreign servers. Public confidence plummeted as users began questioning whether Zoom could be trusted with sensitive information.

Jake shook his head. "They got lucky. The pandemic kept them relevant."

Max laughed. "Maybe, but their proactive response didn't hurt either."

Zoom's response was swift and thorough. They paused feature rollouts to focus entirely on security enhancements, brought in top cybersecurity experts, and launched an intensive 90-day security plan. With transparency at the forefront, Zoom regularly updated users on their progress, sharing detailed changes in real-time and hosting weekly webinars to address questions. This transparency was critical to rebuilding trust, as customers could see the company's commitment to addressing their concerns head-on.

Kim added, "That's internal trust at work. When employees feel empowered to handle crises and understand the company's values, they step up—just like Zoom's team did. Their culture of openness and willingness to learn showed customers they weren't hiding anything."

Eric nodded. "And it paid off. Zoom's relentless focus on security improvements and transparency didn't just address the immediate issues; it strengthened the company's foundation for the long term. By the end of the year, they'd not only regained trust but set a new standard for crisis response in the tech world."

Marcella moved to the final slide. "And there's Sephora. They combined AI-driven personalization with human consultants for a seamless customer experience. Their tech builds trust by making customers feel known—not just like data points."

Eric crossed his arms. "Speed and transparency are key, but we can't forget the human touch."

Jake finally chuckled. "Great, so we just need to be tech-savvy, charitable, authentic, and flawless under pressure. Easy."

Max smirked. "Oh, and human, too."

Marcella leaned against the table. "Exactly. Now let's get practical."

Craft Your Leadership Trust Strategy

Marcella moved to the whiteboard and drew three interconnected circles. "Here's our social proof strategy," she began.

Build Trust (Offensive Plays)

"First, we establish social proof credibility," she explained:

- User content verification programs
- Social proof integration systems
- Customer advocacy initiatives

Protect Trust (Defensive Plays)

Moving to the second circle:

- Content authenticity monitoring
- Review verification protocols
- Advocacy protection measures

Measure Trust

For the final circle:

Trust Metric	Current	Target
Social Proof Impact	70%	90%
Content Authenticity	75%	95%
Customer Advocacy	68%	85%

"Remember," she concluded, "authentic social proof drives lasting trust."

Action Plan for Trust Hacking and Social Proof

Marcella assigned tasks to the team, each aligned with building customer and employee trust through AI-driven personalization, transparency, and user-generated content.

1. AI-Driven Personalization

- *Objective:* Build trust through personalized customer experiences.
- *Tactic:* Use AI to analyze behavior and create tailored content.

"Max, you and Marketing will lead the personalization initiative. Launch it within the next 60 days."

Max grinned. "We'll make every customer feel like we know them—without creeping them out."

2. **Radical Transparency**

    - *Objective:* Build trust by being fully transparent about operations.
    - *Tactic*: Launch a transparency campaign inspired by Patagonia's supply chain model.

"Eric, you'll spearhead this with your team. Rollout plan in 45 days."

Eric nodded. "We'll show everything—the good, the bad, and the fixes."

3. **Internal Trust Alignment**

    - *Objective:* Strengthen internal culture to ensure employees embody trust externally.
    - *Tactic:* "Kim, work with HR to integrate trust metrics into performance reviews and training."

Kim smiled. "Trust starts with the team. If employees feel supported, it trickles down to customers."

4. **Social Proof and User-Generated Content (UGC)**

    o *Objective*: Make customers our best marketers through social proof.
    o *Tactic:* Verified reviews, a hashtag campaign, and content moderation using the GUARDIAN Framework.

Max shared his notes. "We'll build a verified review system, launch a branded hashtag, and set guidelines to keep content on-brand. GUARDIAN principles give us a roadmap: guide, authenticate, and moderate."

A month later, they reconvened to discuss the results.

- Max reported, "AI personalization boosted engagement by 25%. Customers love the tailored experiences."
- Eric added, "Our transparency campaign lifted loyalty by 15%. People respect our openness."
- Kim shared, "Internal trust scores are up 18%. Employees feel aligned with the mission, which shows in customer interactions."
- Jake, who had been skeptical, finally nodded. "Alright, I'll admit it. The numbers don't lie. We're hacking trust, and it's working."
- Marcella beamed. "We're doing the hard work, smarter. That's how you hack trust—by being real."

Steps for the Strategic Leader for Leveraging Social Proof and UGC Aligned with GUARDIAN Principles:

1. **Create a Verified Review System:** Verified reviews add credibility to customer feedback, ensuring potential customers trust the authenticity of what's being said about your product.
2. **Launch a User-Generated Content (UGC) Campaign:** UGC creates authenticity, a core value in GUARDIAN. Customers are more likely to trust content created by other users than corporate ads or brand-driven content.
3. **Establish Content Moderation Guidelines:** Allowing free creative expression can be risky, but with proper moderation, you can highlight the best content while ensuring it aligns with GUARDIAN principles.

By implementing these strategies with GUARDIAN as a foundation, you'll foster a sense of community and harness your customers' power to promote your brand authentically.

7. Trust and Social Media: Managing Online Reputations in a Distrustful Age

"Trust is a currency; you can't afford not to invest in it."

- Juliana Vergara, Altus Growth Partners.

Kim's office was humming with tension. A string of heated online criticisms about Rezilify's latest update was buzzing across social channels, casting a shadow on the brand's reputation. Kim scrolled through Twitter, Reddit threads, and even Glassdoor reviews, her brow furrowing as she scanned the posts. It was clear that this wasn't just typical trolling—this was dissatisfaction reaching a boiling point.

In the past, these issues might have been ignored or minimized, but Kim knew better. Left unchecked, this wave of negativity could damage Rezilify's reputation, not just among customers but also among employees, undermining recruitment and retention efforts.

Without delay, she texted Max and Eric, asking them to meet in her office. Moments later, Max arrived, his face reflecting her concern. "What's up, Kim?"

"This isn't looking good," Kim started. "Our online reputation is taking a hit, and if we don't address this quickly, it'll bleed into our recruitment and overall brand image."

Max nodded, fully aware of the stakes. "Social media's a wildfire—if we don't put it out fast, it could consume everything we've built."

They were mid-discussion when Marcella entered, holding a tablet with the latest metrics. "I'm glad you're all here," she said, paging Jake to join. Our brand sentiment score dropped 35% over the past two months. Viral customer complaints are hitting hard, and we're behind on response times. We're in dangerous territory here."

Marcella shared more eye-opening data. "Our current trust ratings across platforms are uneven at best," she explained. "LinkedIn holds the highest trust with B2B buyers at 89%, but platforms like Facebook are struggling, sitting at a mere 38%. And emerging platforms like BeReal and Threads are showing a 56% higher trust rate among Gen Z than traditional social media options."

Emerging Platform Trends in 2024

1. **TikTok's Rise in B2B Engagement:** TikTok has become a significant player in B2B trust-building, with 45% of decision-makers now using the platform to research vendors. Brands that engage authentically on TikTok see higher trust ratings compared to more traditional platforms.

2. **Gen Z Preference for New Platforms:** Emerging platforms like BeReal and Threads are showing a 56% higher trust rate among Gen Z compared to established social media options. These platforms emphasize authenticity and real-time sharing, resonating well with younger audiences.
3. **Shift Towards Visual and Short-Form Content:** As users increasingly prefer bite-sized, engaging content, platforms that support short-form videos and visual storytelling (like Instagram Reels and TikTok) are gaining traction. Brands are adapting their strategies to create more dynamic, visually appealing content.
4. **Community-Driven Verification:** Platforms are integrating features that allow users to participate in the fact-checking process. This community engagement fosters a sense of trust and transparency, making users feel more involved in the content they consume.
5. **AI Integration:** AI is playing a dual role in content creation and monitoring. While it helps generate content and analyze trends, its involvement also necessitates clear disclosure to maintain trust. Brands are prioritizing transparency about AI usage to build credibility.

Jake arrived, taking in Marcella's tone and the figures on her tablet. "I didn't think the fallout would be this intense," he remarked, watching Marcella swipe to display a viral video with a caption that read,

"Is this what we're paying for?" It had over 100,000 views. He visibly paled at the number.

"This is why we need to act now," Kim said, urgency lacing her voice. "Customers are feeling unheard, and if they keep feeling abandoned, so will our employees."

Marcella continued, pointing at another graph. "AI has changed the game as well. It's both our biggest risk and our greatest opportunity. Right now, 42% of users can't even distinguish between AI-generated and human-created content, which is leading to a significant 35% decrease in brand trust when AI's involvement isn't disclosed."

Max raised an eyebrow, visibly concerned. "So, it's not just about what we say, but how we say it—and whether we're upfront about AI's role in that."

Marcella nodded. "Precisely. People want transparency; 67% of users want clear AI disclosure, and 89% prefer human-made content for sensitive topics. When we're upfront about AI usage, engagement goes up by 45%."

Eric nodded, already shifting into a strategic mode. "We're going to follow the GUARDIAN framework to cover our bases here. This means we'll focus on Growth, User Experience, Audience Centric Analytics, Reputation Management, Digital Brand Authority, Innovative Engagement, Adaptive Marketing, and Network Effect Amplification."

Marcella was on board immediately. "So, let's break this down into actionable steps," she said, noting that the team had successfully leveraged similar strategies in past situations. "This won't just be about damage control; it's about building lasting trust."

Craft Your Leadership Trust Strategy

Marcella drew three interconnected circles. "Let's map our social media trust strategy," she began.

Build Trust (Offensive Plays)

"First, we establish social credibility," she explained:

- Social reputation monitoring
- Community engagement programs
- Content authenticity systems

Protect Trust (Defensive Plays)

Moving to the second circle:

- Social listening protocols
- Crisis response systems
- Reputation protection measures

Measure Trust

For the final circle:

Trust Metric	Current	Target
Social Trust	70%	90%
Response Time	30 min	15 min
Community Engagement	65%	85%

"Remember," Marcella concluded, "social trust is built in minutes but can be lost in seconds."

Social Media Trust Strategy

1. Real-Time Engagement Team

- *Objective:* Reduce social media response times to under an hour.
- *Tactic:* Set up a 24/7 social media team.

"Max, I want this team up and running in 30 days."

Max jotted it down. "We'll be lightning-fast. No more long waits."

2. Social Listening Tools

- o *Objective: Monitor brand sentiment in real time.*
- o *Tactic: Implement a social listening tool to track all mentions of Rezilify.*

"Eric, you'll handle this. We need to catch fires before they spread."

Eric tapped at his keyboard. "I'll get the tool integrated and report back."

3. Crisis Management Protocol

- o *Objective: Prepare for viral situations before they spiral.*
- o *Tactic: Create a crisis protocol with pre-approved messaging.*

"Jake, you and Kim will collaborate on this. Make sure the social media team is trained to handle crises in real-time."

Kim nodded. "We'll train the team on empathy-based responses. It's not just about reacting fast—it's about reacting right."

* * * *

Thirty days later, the team gathered again to review the outcomes of their initiatives. Max was the first to share. "By clearly labeling AI-generated content, engagement went up by 45%—people really appreciated the transparency."

Eric chimed in, "Our social listening tool helped us prevent at least three potential PR disasters by catching complaints early. Real-time tracking dropped our response time to an average of 22 minutes, and incidents of misinformation fell by 67%."

Kim noted that the emphasis on empathy had a strong internal effect. "Employee morale has improved. Our team feels empowered, and we've seen a 45% increase in employee advocacy as they're more confident to stand behind the brand."

Even Jake, typically the skeptic, acknowledged the success. "Trust does have measurable ROI. Our response times and reputation scores are both up significantly, all while staying within budget."

Marcella summarized, "This is what happens when you trust the process. We're not just putting out fires; we're building relationships."

The team learned that trust is a constant, strategic pursuit in the evolving digital landscape of 2024. By turning Rezilify's social media from a reactive channel into a proactive tool, they protected and amplified trust, transforming potential threats into a powerful advantage.

Steps for the Strategic Leader to Manage Social Media Trust:

1. **Build a Real-Time Engagement Team**: In the fast-paced world of social media, delayed responses can amplify customer frustration. A quick, thoughtful reply builds confidence in your brand's commitment to listening and solving issues.
2. **Utilize Social Listening Tools:** By staying ahead of conversations about your brand, you can prevent small issues from turning into major PR crises. Social listening allows you to understand customer sentiment and intervene proactively.
3. **Create a Crisis Management Protocol:** Every brand will face negative feedback at some point, but a well-prepared crisis management plan can prevent damage and even strengthen your reputation by showing accountability.
4. **Implement Empathy in Your Responses:** Customers don't just want fast responses—they want to feel understood. Acknowledging their concerns and addressing them with genuine empathy can turn a negative interaction into a positive experience.
5. **Foster Proactive Community Engagement:** Building a loyal, engaged community can help amplify positive messages about your brand. A proactive approach creates brand advocates who will defend and promote your business organically.

Building lasting trust with your customers and employees enhances your brand and is key to long-term success in the age of digital communication.

8. Why Trust is Becoming Increasingly Crucial in the Digital Age for Brands

"Contrary to what most people believe, trust is not some soft, illusive quality that you either have or you don't; rather, trust is a pragmatic, tangible, actionable asset that you can create."

- Stephen Covey.

As the meeting wrapped up, Kim quickly gathered her notes, glancing over at Max. He was heading toward the door, deep in thought. She hurried to catch up, falling into step with him as they exited the conference room.

"Max, tell me more about this transparency thing," she began. "I get it, but do you really think customers care that much about what goes on behind the scenes? How transparent is too transparent?"

Max gave her a quick sideways glance as they walked, his brow furrowed in thought. "Care? They expect it. It's not just about making them happy anymore, Kim. Customers are like employees; they want to know everything—where their data's going, how we're protecting it, and what happens if something goes wrong. Trust is the new currency. You know that."

Why Trust is Becoming Increasingly Crucial in the Digital Age for Brands

They reached the elevator, and Kim pressed the button. "I know that makes sense. But it feels like trust is so fragile these days. One mistake, and it all falls apart."

Max nodded as they stepped into the elevator. "Exactly. That's why we need to stay ahead of it. We can't just plan to react when things go wrong—we've got to build that trust foundation now before anything happens."

As the elevator doors slid shut, Jake slipped in at the last moment, joining them. "You two talking about trust again?" he asked with a wry smile.

Max leaned back against the elevator wall. "That's all I've been thinking about. We've got the systems in place, but we're not showing our customers that they can trust us with their data and their privacy. It's like we're still hiding behind the curtain."

Jake crossed his arms, nodding slowly. "Trust in the financial world has always been a balancing act. But now? With all the data breaches and misinformation? It's not just about doing the right thing—it's about making sure everyone knows we're doing the right thing."

Kim glanced between the two men, considering their words. "So, transparency, responsiveness, ethics—it all ties together, huh? But how do we make that message land with our customers? It's not enough to just say we're trustworthy."

The elevator slowed to a halt, and Jake answered as the doors opened. "We've got to prove it. That

Don't Believe the Hype

GUARDIAN Framework will definitely help align this. Transparency isn't just a buzzword. It's about showing our customers everything—what we're doing to protect them, how fast we respond, what our ethical stance is. If we're not the ones controlling that narrative, someone else will be."

As they exited the elevator and walked toward their respective offices, Max added, "And that's why we need to be bold. That transparency dashboard we've launched? It's going to give customers a real-time view of everything. No smoke and mirrors, no hiding. Just straight data."

Kim nodded but was concerned. "And you're sure that's not going to backfire? What if something goes wrong?"

Max shrugged. "That's the risk we take. But that's how we build trust, by being upfront—especially when things go wrong."

"Ok, I see it," Kim added, her tone thoughtful. "It's a new kind of relationship with customers. They don't just want reassurance—they want proof. It's like building trust with employees. If you aren't transparent, they'll start filling in the gaps with their ideas—and that's never good."

Jake gave a small smile. "Exactly. The more open we are, the more control we have over the narrative. One mistake might set us back, but covering it up? That's a death sentence."

Max stopped at his office door, turning to face them both. "And that's the difference between surviving in this digital world and leading it. We're not just managing expectations—we're setting them. If we make trust a priority now, we'll be light years ahead of the competition."

Kim smiled. "I like it. It's not just about playing defense anymore."

Jake raised his hand in a mock salute as he headed off. "Let's just make sure we've got the numbers to back it all up. Trust may be built on transparency, but our future depends on making that trust profitable."

Max watched as Jake walked away, then glanced at Kim. "We're laying the foundation here, Kim. Every decision we make, every step we take toward transparency, responsiveness, and governance—it's all going to pay off. And by fully implementing the GUARDIAN Framework, we're building trust that will last."

Kim nodded, the weight of the conversation settling in. "And if we do it right, we won't just keep up with the digital age. We'll define it."

Max smiled. "That's the plan."

As they parted ways, the gravity of their task hung in the air. Trust wasn't just a challenge—it was the key to their future success. In a world where skepticism reigned, transparency, responsiveness, and ethics would be their guideposts. The foundation of their digital trust ecosystem was being built, and now it was time to ensure it was unshakable.

9. Trust by the Numbers - Core Stats that Define the Trust Economy

In God we trust; all others must bring data."

— W. Edwards Deming.

Jake leaned back in his chair after disconnecting from his weekly CFO leadership call. The theme of trust dominated the conversation, surfacing in every data point and market trend discussed. As he rubbed his temples, replaying the key takeaways, he heard a light knock on the doorframe.

"Busy?" Eric asked, stepping in without waiting for an answer.

Jake gestured to the chair in front of his desk. "Just finished. Got a lot to think about from this CFO call, but trust me, it was all about numbers and trust—surprise, surprise."

Eric chuckled as he took a seat. "Seems like that's all anyone talks about these days. So, what did they say?"

Jake pulled up his notes, glancing over the key data points as he shared the highlights with Eric. "Trust isn't just a buzzword anymore. It's a bona fide economic driver. The companies that are winning?

They're the ones weaving digital trust into every interaction—from blockchain transparency to secure metaverse environments. Trust has become currency."

Eric crossed his arms, intrigued. "Makes sense. We've been talking about it internally for a while now, but it sounds like the market's finally catching up."

"Yeah, and here's the kicker—trust isn't just a soft metric anymore; it's measurable, and it's showing up with real influence on the bottom line," Jake replied, scanning the stats. "For example, businesses with high trust ratings see a 30% higher customer retention rate, and 83% of consumers said they'd stop purchasing from brands they no longer trust."

Eric raised an eyebrow. "People are willing to pay a premium just to feel secure? That's huge. It makes it all so much more tangible."

Jake nodded. "And it doesn't stop there. B2B metrics are shifting, too. Do you know that 75% of B2B buyers now require vendor trust before even considering engagement? 90% value transparency in pricing and contracts above other factors. Blockchain is a big part of that shift, offering verifiable records that help assure them."

Eric leaned forward. "That's brutal. But it tracks. Remember those significant breaches with EquiLend, Microsoft, Tencent, and Dell over 2023 and 2024? Cybersecurity trust alone dropped by 12%, and cloud providers have seen a 15% drop due to privacy concerns. Blockchain is still emerging, but the brands using it are getting a trust boost."

"Exactly," Jake continued. "A recent study showed that companies investing proactively in trust-building—data security, transparency, governance, even blockchain-based verifications—see an average of 20% higher revenue growth. And here's a new stat: 85% of investors are prioritizing companies with strong governance frameworks."

Eric let out a low whistle. "That's practically the entire market saying trust is the future. And we're already seeing it here, right? Our customers are demanding more transparency and more accountability. The days of 'just trust us' are over."

Jake's voice grew more animated. "Here's a hard reality: companies that lose trust can face a 5% drop in market value immediately after a trust-related scandal. Recovery isn't guaranteed; it can take years to regain ground. Our job isn't just to avoid those losses but to actively demonstrate that we're the most trustworthy option."

Eric scratched his chin, thoughtful. "That makes it all the more important that we stay ahead of the curve. We're implementing Borenstein's GUARDIAN Digital Trust Framework™, but what'll really set us apart is proving we're trustworthy from the outset—not just reacting to issues."

Jake leaned back, a satisfied expression on his face. "Trust may seem like an emotional concept, but it's deeply rooted in hard numbers. North American market trust in tech sits at 65%, but in Europe, it's down to 55%. That's a huge opportunity for us to lead on trust and take market share."

Eric leaned back, impressed. "I knew trust mattered, but I didn't realize it was directly tied to growth. We're really talking about market share."

Jake nodded. "And customer satisfaction, too. Companies with high-trust ratings? They have an 85% retention rate, compared to just 45% for low-trust companies. We're talking about long-term loyalty driven as much by trust as by product quality."

"So, what's our next move?" Eric asked with a gleam of excitement in his eye.

Jake thought for a moment. "First, we need to start quantifying our trust metrics. Investors, customers—everyone wants proof now. Let's integrate trust-related KPIs into our reporting. Things like response times for customer issues, transparency metrics, and blockchain verifications."

Eric nodded. "We're tightening the AI service platform to ensure faster escalations. Maybe we could incorporate customer satisfaction scores tied directly to those response times to show that we're not just responding but solving problems faster than the competition."

Jake raised a finger. "And our ethical governance initiatives? Let's make those resonate with investors. Our first ethics report needs to do more than check a box. We have to show we're not just protecting data; we're making every digital interaction above board."

Just then, Marcella entered and settled in with them. "I see we're getting detailed on our approach to B2B trust, but we need to carry that rigor over to B2C as well. While B2B is driven by consistency and expertise, remember that B2C trust depends heavily on building emotional connections."

Jake nodded. "For B2C, it's about transparency, control, and engagement." He pulled up insights grounded in the GUARDIAN Framework:

Authenticity and Transparency (G, T):

- 86% of consumers prefer brands that disclose product sourcing and sustainability.
- 72% of B2C consumers feel more loyal to brands that are transparent about data usage.

User Experience and Engagement (U, E):

- Engaging user experiences leads to 42% higher satisfaction among B2C customers.
- Personalized experiences, like Nike Fit, build trust by addressing real-life needs.

Community and Emotional Bonds (A, N):

- Strong brand communities increase retention by 32%.
- Community-driven content can amplify trust by 53% in B2C spaces.

Marcella summarized, "We're looking at creating a brand experience where every interaction feels meaningful. B2C customers need to feel valued, not just informed. That's what builds emotional loyalty."

Jake nodded. "Our trust-building strategy has to go beyond product and service quality—it's about a brand relationship that resonates."

Eric slapped his leg as he stood up and walked to the whiteboard. "Well, it sounds like we've got our work cut out for us. But if we nail this, we're not just future-proofing Rezilify—we're positioning ourselves as leaders in the trust economy."

Craft Your Leadership Trust Strategy

Eric drew three interconnected circles. "Here's our trust metrics blueprint," he began.

Build Trust (Offensive Plays)

"First, we establish metrics credibility," he explained:

- Trust measurement systems
- Data transparency programs
- Performance tracking protocols

Protect Trust (Defensive Plays)

Moving to the second circle:

- Metrics verification systems
- Data integrity checks
- Performance monitoring measures

Measure Trust

For the final circle:

Trust Metric	Current	Target
Trust Score	70%	90%
Data Integrity	75%	95%
Performance Rating	68%	85%

"Remember," Eric concluded, "what gets measured gets managed."

Steps for the Strategic Leader to Evaluate Core Stats:

1. **Quantify Trust Metrics:** Establish KPIs related to trust, such as response times for customer issues, data breach prevention measures, and ethical decision-making processes. Track and report these metrics transparently to build customer and investor confidence.
2. **Prioritize Governance and Transparency:** Implement and publicize ethical governance practices and data security

measures to ensure trustworthiness in all digital interactions. Share these practices in reports to appeal to investors and stakeholders.
3. **Invest in Trust-Building Initiatives**: Proactively invest in initiatives like transparency frameworks, data protection, and customer service improvements. These investments can lead to higher customer retention, revenue growth, and investor confidence.
4. **Monitor and Adapt:** Continuously track trust-related metrics and be prepared to adjust strategies in response to data, ensuring your company stays ahead in the trust economy.

10. The Main Challenges Businesses Faced Related to the Decline of Trust in 2023 – 2024

Trust is like the air we breathe—when it's present, nobody notices; when it's absent, everyone does."

— Warren Buffett.

The conference room buzzed with the low hum of chatter as the Rezilify team gathered for their monthly strategy meeting. It had been a challenging few months, with everyone working overtime to understand and stem the tide of eroding consumer trust and implement the GUARDIAN Framework. But today's meeting was different. This wasn't just a typical strategy session; this was about survival on a very basic level. Trust in businesses had plummeted across industries, and now it was their job to ensure that Rezilify didn't become another casualty.

At the head of the table, Marcella stood ready. Sharp as ever, she tapped the screen to life, silencing the room as the meeting agenda appeared. At the top of the list: "The Trust Crisis—2023-2024 Recap & Next Steps."

She didn't waste any time. "Team, we need to address the growing elephant in the room—consumer

The Main Challenges Businesses Faced Related to the decline of Trust in 2023-2024

trust. The numbers for 2023-2024 are in, and frankly, they're worse than we anticipated."

Max leaned forward. "How bad are we talking, Marcella?"

Marcella pulled up the presentation, filled with grim charts and steep declines. "Consumer trust is sitting at just 51%, down from 61% two years ago. And here's the kicker: I know we throw this around a lot, but 83% of consumers still say they would stop purchasing from a brand they no longer trust. Still."

"I know," Jake winced, rubbing his forehead. "That's a massive hit to the bottom line. Trying to work out the financial implications in real time would be a nightmare."

"It's not just us or cybersecurity, though," Eric added. "Across industries, trust is collapsing. Customers are more skeptical than ever. It's like they're waiting for us to mess up."

"And they aren't shy about sharing their opinions either. Glassdoor, Indeed, social media—all it takes is one bad experience, and the reputation damage spirals." Kim sighed.

Marcella's voice remained steady but firm. "Exactly. The real challenge is figuring out how we stop this decline before it really affects us and avoid becoming another statistic."

Max stared at the charts, deep in thought. "What changed now though? Why are we seeing this across the board?"

Marcella flipped to the next slide. "There are a few culprits—data breaches, misinformation, and corporate scandals—each breach, every public misstep over the entire industry, chips away at general consumer trust. People no longer assume companies act in their best interests. They think businesses are only out for themselves."

Eric jumped in, already strategizing. "Sounds familiar. Remember the Meta fiasco in 2023? They were under constant scrutiny over privacy issues, and public trust was hitting rock bottom. They had to double down on transparency and user safety just to claw back some trust."

He elaborated, recalling how Meta, the parent company of Facebook and Instagram, faced an unrelenting series of privacy controversies in 2023. Reports surfaced that sensitive user data was being collected and shared with third parties without clear user consent, leading to outrage among consumers and criticism from privacy advocates. As more details came to light, the media spotlight intensified, highlighting Meta's perceived lack of regard for user privacy and fueling a growing movement for stricter data protection.

"Meta was in a tight spot," Eric continued. "Their user base was questioning whether their data was safe, and advertisers were starting to pull back, not wanting to be associated with a platform under fire."

To address the crisis, Meta had to act decisively. They launched a comprehensive initiative focused on transparency and user safety, implementing new privacy tools that allowed users to control how their data was used more effectively. Meta also started publishing regular reports detailing their privacy practices, providing clear explanations on how user data was being handled. They opened a series of town hall meetings to hear directly from users about their privacy concerns, a move that signaled a commitment to listening and improving.

"Meta's actions weren't just about damage control," Eric noted. "They needed to show they were genuinely changing. They went as far as updating their algorithms to limit data sharing and even hired a third-party auditor to evaluate their data practices."

The measures helped Meta make incremental gains in user trust, though the recovery was slow and still ongoing. By prioritizing transparency and user control, Meta managed to retain a significant portion of their audience. But the incident served as a stark reminder of how quickly trust could erode—and how challenging it was to rebuild.

"It's a great example of what happens when trust is compromised," Eric concluded. "Meta had to go beyond quick fixes. They needed a full-scale, transparent strategy just to start regaining user confidence."

Max nodded. "That's the key here—transparency. They turned things around by being upfront, but it wasn't a quick fix."

Marcella looked around the table. "We need to act now. Sitting back and hoping trust rebuilds itself across the board isn't an option. We're going to focus on three key areas: Transparency, Crisis Response, and Actionable Guarantees. We have to lead the charge, not just for ourselves but all digital companies. People need to believe that we are worthy of their trust." She clicked on another slide titled "Key Strategies for Rebuilding Trust."

1. Transparency and Open Communication

"Max, you're leading this," Marcella said, nodding toward him. "We need a campaign that clearly outlines how we handle customer data and why customers can trust us. Think of Meta's 2023 pivot. They laid everything out in the open, and that transparency worked. Customers knew exactly what was happening with their data."

Max straightened up, already brainstorming. "I'll work with IT and legal to make sure we craft something clear, something people actually understand. We need to reassure customers that their data is safe with us."

"Make sure it's not too technical," Eric added with a smirk. "People tune out after the first five acronyms."

Kim raised an eyebrow. "And don't forget employees. Internally, we need to make sure everyone knows what to say when customers start asking questions. Consistency is key."

"Good thinking, Kim," Marcella nodded toward her, "I'd like you to take that one."

The Main Challenges Businesses Faced Related to the decline of Trust in 2023-2024

2. Customer-Centric Crisis Response

Next, Marcella turned to Eric. "We've seen what happens when companies don't get ahead of crises. Trust tanks and it's nearly impossible to recover. We need a crisis communication plan that addresses issues immediately and transparently."

"Definitely." Eric nodded, already thinking ahead. "We can't be reactive. Think Johnson & Johnson with the vaccine concerns during COVID. They owned their mistakes, communicated early, and customers respected them for it."

"Exactly," Marcella said. "We need to model that. When something goes wrong—and it will—we've got to be the first to tell our customers, not the last."

3. Actionable Guarantees for Restoring Trust

Finally, Marcella looked at Jake, her expression resolute. "Jake, we need guarantees. Apologies aren't enough when it comes to security issues. Microsoft's response after their 2023 breach is a prime example. They didn't just issue an apology; they backed it up with tangible, actionable guarantees. That's what restored trust."

She continued, describing Microsoft's approach to handling a severe data breach that had rocked the tech world in 2023. In the wake of the breach, users and clients were understandably skeptical about the security of Microsoft's products and data handling practices. But Microsoft took swift and concrete action to address these concerns head-on. Instead of vague reassurances, they launched a series of product guarantees designed to reinforce their commitment to security.

"Microsoft didn't just talk," Marcella emphasized. "They offered certifications and warranties on their software to prove that their systems were up to the highest security standards. They went through rigorous third-party audits, certified by top cybersecurity firms, and ensured that every step in their recovery plan was documented and verifiable."

This comprehensive approach was not only proactive but customer-centric. Microsoft provided clients with the option to receive independent security audits for high-risk accounts and offered a guarantee that, in the event of a future breach, affected clients would receive immediate support and compensation. By delivering these assurances, Microsoft transformed a potential disaster into an opportunity to rebuild credibility and restore user confidence.

Jake nodded, beginning to understand the impact of these steps. "So they didn't just fix the problem—they actively proved to their customers that they'd made changes and could be trusted again."

"Exactly," Marcella replied. "They realized that trust isn't just about fixing what's broken; it's about preventing future issues and making customers feel secure. Guarantees and certifications show that they're committed to their promises, and that's what makes the difference." Jake sighed but didn't argue. "I get it. Guarantees are fine, but I'll need to work out

The Main Challenges Businesses Faced Related to the decline of Trust in 2023-2024

how this impacts the bottom line. Certifications aren't cheap."

"Trust isn't cheap either," Max shot back, half-joking but with an edge. "You want numbers, right? Well, people are more likely to buy from certified brands they trust, and they'll pay a premium for it. It's an investment."

Jake smirked. "Touché, but I'll need to see the ROI. I'll map out a plan and look at a few digital trust certification programs, but it's got to make financial sense."

Marcella nodded. "We'll make it work. We're potentially on a slippery slope, and realistically, we have about 90 days to start turning this around. Max, your transparency campaign needs to go live within 30 days. Kim, you work on consistent employee education. Eric, we need that crisis plan locked down in 60 days. And Jake, your product guarantees and certifications need to be in place by the 90-day mark."

The room was silent for a moment, the weight of the challenge ahead sinking in. Once lost, trust was hard to regain. There was another dimension to it almost weekly. But the team knew they had the tools and strategy to make it happen.

Finally, Eric broke the silence with a half-smile. "No pressure, right?"

Kim chuckled. "Pressure makes diamonds. Let's figure this out."

Craft Your Leadership Trust Strategy

Marcella drew three interconnected circles. "Let's map our trust challenges strategy," she began.

Build Trust (Offensive Plays)

"First, we establish challenge mitigation credibility," she explained:

- Trust restoration programs
- Digital credibility initiatives
- Stakeholder engagement systems

Protect Trust (Defensive Plays)

Moving to the second circle:

- Challenge monitoring protocols
- Trust protection measures
- Crisis prevention systems

The Main Challenges Businesses Faced Related to the decline of Trust in 2023-2024

Measure Trust

For the final circle:

Trust Metric	Current	Target
Trust Score	70%	90%
Challenge Resolution	75%	95%
Stakeholder Trust	68%	85%

"Remember," Marcella concluded, "challenges are opportunities to strengthen trust."

Steps for the Strategic Leader to Overcome the Main Challenges in Business:

1. **Increase Transparency** – Implement clear, digestible communication about how your business handles customer data and ensures privacy. Educate both customers and employees to ensure consistency.
2. **Proactive Crisis Management:** Develop a crisis response plan that emphasizes transparency and immediate action.

Acknowledge mistakes quickly to maintain trust.
3. **Offer Actionable Guarantees** – Rebuild trust with concrete promises, such as certifications, guarantees, or product assurances that back up your claims.
4. **Measure Trust** – Regularly track key metrics related to customer trust, such as satisfaction scores, retention rates, and public sentiment.

11. The Biggest Challenges Marketers Face in Building and Maintaining Trust in the Digital Age

Content builds relationships; relationships are built on trust. Trust drives revenue.

- Andrew Davis

Max's office was flooded with the soft afternoon light filtering through the floor-to-ceiling windows, offering a calming view of the city skyline. Inside, however, the atmosphere was anything but calm. Max sat at his desk, tapping his fingers on the keyboard as he stared at the screen in front of him. His office was the usual spot for impromptu brainstorming sessions. Today, he was joined by Eric and Jake as they figured out their deliverables from the recent strategy meeting with Marcella.

Max leaned back, sighing. "The trust thing ... It's getting more complicated by the day. The more we know, the more we see we don't know. How did something that should be so basic become so complicated, detailed, and fragile?"

Lounging on Max's couch with his usual nonchalance, Eric smirked. "Because nothing is ever basic when you add humans to the equation, Max.

Trust is about perception. One misstep, and you've got a mountain to climb."

Jake clasped his hands together. "I hear you both, but let's talk about the bottom line. Trust issues hit revenue directly. If we lose consumer confidence, we're losing money. It's that simple."

Max exhaled loudly. "No, it's not that simple. It's deeper than just numbers and perception. There's this constant demand for transparency, but too much of it can backfire. You give customers every little detail, and suddenly they're questioning why we feel the need to explain so much."

Eric grinned. "Ah, the 'Transparency Paradox.' Isn't that what Marcella called it the other day? The more you reveal, the more they wonder what you're hiding."

"And we have to balance that? Sounds like a nightmare." Jake rolled his eyes. Max nodded, leaning forward. "Exactly. Too little information, and you're secretive. Too much, and you overwhelm them, and trust starts to erode. It's a fine balance, and I've been looking at some big brands trying to manage this—let me tell you, it's messy."

He paused, pulling up an example on the screen. "Take Apple's situation back in 2023. They'd had a strong run with their privacy campaigns, branding themselves as champions of user data protection. Their marketing was all about security and transparency, which built a lot of goodwill with their customers."

The Biggest Challenges Marketers Face in Building and Maintaining Trust in the Digital Age

But, as Max explained, the spotlight on Apple's privacy practices inadvertently shone a light on other aspects of their business. Questions started surfacing around their supply chain ethics, environmental impact, and labor practices, especially regarding the production of Apple devices overseas. The more the public looked, the more they began to question the consistency of Apple's values.

"Apple was transparent, but only about certain aspects," Max continued. "They were clear about privacy, but they hadn't been as open with other parts of their operations. And that created room for doubt. People felt there was more Apple wasn't saying, and that gap gave the media an opening."

The coverage quickly snowballed, with journalists and advocacy groups scrutinizing Apple's labor practices, carbon footprint, and sourcing ethics. Customers who had trusted Apple for their privacy standards started wondering if the company was selective with its transparency. The doubts cast a shadow over Apple's commitment to its values, and the brand's carefully constructed image began to show cracks.

Eric leaned in, understanding the nuance. "So, even though they were transparent in some areas, the lack of clarity in others created a perception that they were hiding something."

"Exactly," Max said. "Apple's transparency around privacy was strong, but by not addressing these other areas head-on, they left space for skepticism. That's where trust can falter—when customers feel they're only getting part of the story."

Jake folded his arms, skeptical as always. "So, where's the sweet spot? How much transparency is enough without tipping the scales?"

Max turned his screen toward them, showing a few other case studies. "Take Nike as another example. They've faced heat for their labor practices, but instead of releasing every single piece of data, they focused on the key things that their consumers care about—environmental impact, fair wages, and community building. They gave just enough information to show they were addressing the issues, but not so much that it invited unnecessary scrutiny."

Eric scratched his chin. "Strategic transparency, then. Enough to build trust, but not so much that it blows up in your face."

"Exactly. And we need to figure out how to do the same. We've already faced data transparency challenges this year. Transparency's going to be a big deal in our next product launch."

Jake sighed, leaning back in his chair. "So what's the solution, Max? We can't afford a misstep here. What are you proposing?"

Max stood up, pacing. "Here's what we need to do, and it's going to be a three-pronged approach." He had a thousand-yard stare and started outlining his plan, counting on his fingers. "First, we need to implement blockchain as part of our transparency plan. By using blockchain technology, we can verify every significant

The Biggest Challenges Marketers Face in Building and Maintaining Trust in the Digital Age

data point in real time, creating a trusted record that's visible to customers and auditors alike. This way, we're not just saying 'trust us'; we're backing it up with irrefutable data."

Eric nodded, intrigued. "So blockchain gives us a solid foundation for transparency without overwhelming people with the nitty-gritty. They can verify details, but we control the scope."

"Exactly," Max agreed. "The second prong is making information digestible. We have these dashboards and customer portals, but we need them to be intuitive. People don't want to sift through pages of jargon. They want quick, accessible insights. Like Tesla's transparency dashboards on car performance and data privacy. It's interactive but simple."

Jake, finally convinced, nodded. "That makes sense. What's the third prong?"

Max turned to Jake. "Employee advocacy. If we want our transparency plan to succeed, it has to start from within. We need to ensure that every employee understands our trust metrics and feels empowered to communicate that transparency with customers directly. If they're on board, they're our best advocates. I'll work with Kim on rolling out an employee advocacy program that trains staff on key transparency metrics and how to address customer concerns on the spot."

Eric raised an eyebrow. "So, it's about training them to handle trust-building directly. Makes sense. If they know the messaging and the reasoning behind it, they won't need to escalate every issue."

Max smiled. "Exactly. Trust starts internally. When our employees trust the processes, they can communicate that confidence to customers."

Jake sighed, rubbing his temples. "Alright, fine. I'll work with Kim on a new training module to integrate that. I'm going to need to see this result in hard numbers, Max."

Max grinned. "You'll see the results, Jake. Trust me."

Craft Your Leadership Trust Strategy

Eric drew three interconnected circles. "Here's our marketing trust blueprint," he began.

Build Trust (Offensive Plays)

"First, we establish marketing credibility," he explained:

- Content authenticity programs
- Marketing transparency initiatives
- Customer engagement systems

Protect Trust (Defensive Plays)

Moving to the second circle:

- Marketing claims verification
- Message consistency checks
- Brand protection measures

The Biggest Challenges Marketers Face in Building and Maintaining Trust in the Digital Age

Measure Trust

For the final circle:

Trust Metric	Current	Target
Marketing Trust	70%	90%
Message Authenticity	75%	95%
Customer Confidence	68%	85%

"Remember," Eric concluded, "marketing trust is earned through consistency and proven through results."

As the two executives stood to leave, Jake looked at Max. "Do you really think this will work?"

Max chuckled. "It has to. The alternative is falling into that transparency paradox, and trust me, none of us want to be there."

"There's no reason it shouldn't," Eric agreed, and then a smirk crept across his face, "We can call it the trident of truth."

Eric clapped Max on the shoulder. "Hey, at least we're smart enough to talk it through before we trip over our own feet."

Max smirked back. "Exactly. Now, let's make sure the rest of the world trusts us as much as we trust each other."

Steps for the Strategic Leader to Maintain Digital Trust:

1. Communicate Transparently, But Stay Focused:

- Develop a communication strategy that focuses on the most critical and relevant information for your customers. Avoid overwhelming them with too much detail.

Audit your current transparency practices and ensure that only clear, valuable information is being shared. Anything beyond that could dilute trust.

2. Leverage Technology to Build Connections, Not Confusion:

- Use tools that simplify complex information. Dashboards, visualizations, and customer portals should be easy to navigate and provide meaningful insights without overloading the user.

Review and streamline your customer-facing technology to ensure it empowers rather than confuses users.

The Biggest Challenges Marketers Face in Building and Maintaining Trust in the Digital Age

3. Empower Employees to Build Trust from Within:

- Equip employees with the knowledge and autonomy they need to handle customer concerns about trust. The more empowered they are, the less likely issues will escalate.

Create or update internal training programs that focus on trust-building practices and transparency goal.

12. What We Trust Depends on the Generation We Come From

"Each generation imagines itself to be more intelligent than the one that went before it and wiser than the one that comes after it."

- George Orwell

Eric leaned back in his office chair, tapping a pen against the table as he looked out the window. There was a stack of papers on the table in front of him. It was a gray, miserable day, and it seemed much later than it was. Kim sat across from him, her arms resting on a stack of reports. Max stood by the whiteboard, arms crossed, grinning as they debated how different generations viewed brands—and trust.

"Alright," Eric began, flipping through the pages in front of him. "We're living in a trust economy now. The way people look at brands is different. Each generation comes with its own set of expectations. So how do we communicate with all of them—equally?"

Kim nodded, leaning forward. "It's not just about what we're saying, but how we're saying it. I've seen this on Glassdoor and in recruitment. What appeals to one generation can alienate another."

What We Trust Depends on the Generation We Come From

Eric smirked. "Boomers want a legacy, Gen X wants efficiency, Millennials want values, and Gen Z—well, they don't even trust the idea of brands anymore."

Max grinned at Eric's bluntness. "That's true. But they still interact with brands, just on their own terms. They follow influencers more than companies. So we have to get creative."

Kim crossed her legs, thinking aloud. "Boomers are used to consistency, right? They grew up with brands that stuck around—Coca-Cola, Ford, IBM. They value long-term reliability and expect us to prove that we're dependable."

"Exactly," Max agreed. "For Baby Boomers, it's about showing up consistently. If we flinch or change too often, we lose them."

Eric chimed in. "Then there's Gen X—our skeptical bunch. They don't care about flashy ads or social causes unless it's tied to results. They just want something that works."

"True," Kim added. "Gen X doesn't want to be sold a dream. They want the facts, delivered efficiently. No fluff, no distractions—just results."

Max leaned forward, scribbling notes. "Millennials, though, are all about authenticity and purpose. They grew up during economic upheaval and the rise of corporate scandals. They need transparency, and they need brands to stand for something real."

Kim nodded again. "Millennials trust companies that align with their values. I've seen it with recruitment. They'll choose a lower salary for a company that shares their social values. If we show that we care—whether it's about the environment, social justice, or employee welfare—they'll buy in."

Eric, always the strategist, interjected. "But Gen Z? They're even more skeptical. They've grown up with access to infinite information and can smell inauthenticity from a mile away. They're all about peer validation and real stories. If a YouTuber or TikTokker says our brand is legit, that's more valuable than a million-dollar ad campaign."

Max smirked. "And that's where we have to get clever. Gen Z doesn't care about carefully curated messages. They want real people—stories that feel raw, unpolished, and relatable. We can't hide behind a polished corporate facade. They want to see the cracks and understand our imperfections."

Kim laughed. "Basically, we need to show them that we're human."

Eric clicked his pen, turning his chair back toward the window. "So how do we pull this off? How do we build trust with Boomers, Gen Xers, Millennials, and Gen Z—without coming off as disjointed?"

Max grabbed the marker and started drawing on the whiteboard. "It's like a four-lane highway. We have to maintain a core message of trust but adapt the delivery to each lane. Boomers need to see legacy and consistency. Gen X needs to hear no-nonsense, results-driven messaging. Millennials need to believe

What We Trust Depends on the Generation We Come From

in our purpose, and Gen Z needs to feel like they're part of our story."

Kim leaned in, her voice steady. "We also need to be careful not to overextend. If we try to be everything to everyone, we'll lose the core of who we are. Our message should remain constant, but how we present it—now that's where the finesse comes in."

Max started sketching out ideas for campaigns that spoke to each generation. "Alright, here's what we'll do. Let's keep our branding consistent but tailored. With Boomers, we emphasize our longevity. For Gen X, we focus on practicality and results. Millennials need to see our social commitment front and center. And Gen Z? We're going to let influencers, real customers, and authentic stories do the talking."

Eric grinned. "That's the play—adapt the communication without losing the integrity of the brand."

Kim added, "And we need to communicate internally, too. Our teams should be aware of this approach so everyone's aligned. If HR, marketing, and strategy aren't all on the same page, this will fail."

Eric stood up, energized. "Alright, let's get to work. Max, start shaping the campaigns and messaging. I'll handle the strategy alignment. Kim, let's make sure the team is looped in and understands how to communicate this trust to our employees as well as our customers."

Kim smiled. "You've got it."

Eric leaned back as the discussion wrapped up, a determined smile crossing his face. "Looks like we've got our work cut out for us. But if we nail this, we'll build trust across the board."

Max nodded, "It's all about the balance. One brand, multiple ways to show trust."

Craft Your Leadership Trust Strategy

Eric drew three interconnected circles. "Here's our generational trust blueprint," he began.

Build Trust (Offensive Plays)

"First, we establish generational credibility," he explained:

- Generation-specific trust programs
- Multi-generational engagement systems
- Targeted value propositions

Protect Trust (Defensive Plays)

Moving to the second circle:

- Generation monitoring protocols
- Cross-generational trust bridges
- Value alignment measures

What We Trust Depends on the Generation We Come From

Measure Trust

For the final circle:

Trust Metric	Current	Target
Gen Z Trust	65%	85%
Millennial Trust	70%	90%
Boomer Trust	75%	95%

"Remember," Eric concluded, "trust speaks different languages across generations."

Steps for the Strategic Leader to Reach Each Generation:

1. Build Consistency for Boomers:

Baby Boomers value reliability. Your brand's messaging should reinforce a long history of success and dependability. Use examples of past achievements to create trust.

2. Deliver Results for Gen X:

Gen X is skeptical and doesn't appreciate fluff. Be straightforward in your communication, focusing on efficiency, value, and precise results.

3. Align with Purpose for Millennials:

Millennials look for brands that reflect their values. Highlight your company's commitment to social responsibility, sustainability, or ethical business practices. Transparency is key.

4. Show Authenticity for Gen Z:

Gen Z prefers raw, real content. To build trust, use authentic storytelling, peer recommendations, and influencer marketing. Avoid overly polished corporate messaging and let real people represent your brand.

PART III: WHAT CAN YOU DO ABOUT IT?

13. Building Trust Through Customer Service in the AI Age

"Customer service shouldn't just be a department; it should be the entire company."

- Eric Hsieh, Founder of Zappos

Rezilify's leadership team reconvened, knowing that customer service was under the microscope. Marcella Rosen, CEO, opened the meeting by reminding them of their goal: integrating AI not just for efficiency but to build trust—a central tenet of Borenstein's GUARDIAN Digital Trust Framework™.

"As it stands, we're lagging in customer service," she began, her tone resolute. "Over half of contact centers—52%—have already invested in Conversational AI, with 44% more planning to adopt AI solutions next year. To build and maintain trust, we need to rethink how we handle customer interactions and ensure the entire system reflects our GUARDIAN principles."

Max Jordan, CMO, nodded. "The market data's clear: 83% of companies transforming their customer experience (CX) with AI are seeing measurable outcomes. We can't afford to fall behind."

Building Trust Through Customer Service in the AI Age

Marcella outlined the latest metrics that underscored the need for action:

- **Primary AI Applications:** Request routing (29%), feedback analysis (28%), and chatbots or self-service tools (26%)—each addressing core needs in CX.
- **Automation Benefits:** 84% of users report improved digital journeys with AI chatbots, 46% experience more personalized interactions, and 48% of service specialists confirm improved response accuracy.
- **24/7 Support:** 36% of experts cite AI's role in constant availability, with time savings (31%) and faster response rates (30%) bolstering customer trust.

She continued, "This isn't just about reducing our load; it's about building trust by giving customers fast, reliable, and consistent service, anytime. This is where we can start actively integrating Borenstein's GUARDIAN Digital Trust Framework™."

Under the GUARDIAN Framework, Rezilify has made significant progress in establishing consistent and transparent customer engagement. With the addition of AI tools, they have the opportunity to take these efforts even further by focusing on the following:

G - Growth Through Authenticity: Leverage AI to guide customers effectively with precise request routing and response accuracy tools, fostering trust and authentic relationships.

U - User Experience Excellence: Enhance the customer journey by understanding feedback through

AI-driven sentiment analysis, leading to personalized and relevant interactions.

A—Audience-Centric Analytics: Use AI to automate routine tasks, allowing agents to focus on complex cases and ensuring consistent service availability and tailored solutions.

R - Reputation Management: Resolve customer issues with greater precision—48% of service specialists report AI improves response accuracy, and companies using AI achieve up to 92% resolution accuracy, boosting reputation.

D - Digital Brand Authority: Be transparent about AI's role in the customer experience, cultivating trust and reinforcing the brand's credibility in the digital space.

I - Innovative Customer Engagement: Continuously innovate by embracing new AI tools and methods to stay ahead in the evolving field of customer experience (CX) transformation.

A - Adaptive Marketing Intelligence: Authenticate interactions through regular audits and fact-checking, ensuring data integrity and reliable insights for strategic decisions.

N - Network Effect Amplification: Use real-time metrics to monitor and improve customer satisfaction, retention, and engagement, driving growth through data-driven insights and optimizing the customer experience.

By aligning AI with these key principles, Rezilify can improve operational efficiency and create more meaningful, personalized experiences that strengthen customer relationships and drive sustainable growth.

Building Trust Through Customer Service in the AI Age

Max offered a strategic view. "We'll route basic inquiries to chatbots—getting that 24/7 availability that's expected today. But our agents should still be empowered to deal with complex issues, using AI insights to provide even more personalized interactions."

Kimberly Rogan, CHRO, observed, "A balanced approach like this aligns with the GUARDIAN framework's advocacy for a human touch in customer service. Our workforce will need to be extensively trained in this Framework—AI isn't here to replace anyone but to enable them."

Measuring Customer Service Trust: Key Metrics for Progress

To track the impact of AI, Marcella proposed using Customer Satisfaction Score (CSAT), Net Promoter Score (NPS), Customer Effort Score (CES), and First Response Time (FRT). "These are the metrics that show how well we're building trust through AI," she explained. "Industry results support this—91% of businesses report satisfaction with AI implementations, 69% note improved customer service, and 55% report reduced wait times and streamlined workflows."

Jake Benjamin, CFO, ran through the expected outcomes. "Financially, we're anticipating significant gains. Streamlined workflows, reduced wait times, and operational cost savings are all part of the ROI of this investment. AI has reduced operational costs by 65% for some firms, with employee productivity rising 35%."

Max pointed out specific AI integration strategies:

Immediate Response Protocol:
AI monitoring for 24/7 customer availability, backed by a human verification team, ensuring all responses meet Borenstein's GUARDIAN Digital Trust Framework's™ quality standards.

Transparency and Accuracy:
A transparent correction policy and rapid fact-checking system to authenticate responses in real time.

Metrics and Real-Time Progress in Building AI-Driven Customer Trust
The team implemented key strategies, integrating AI tools with GUARDIAN's trust-oriented approach. They set clear AI disclosure policies, regular authenticity audits, and community verification systems.

When they met again to assess progress, Marcella began, "Early data shows that AI is making an impact."

Max shared the first results:

- **Operational Metrics:** Average response times were reduced by 60%, resolution time improved by 45%, customer satisfaction rose by 28%, and employee productivity increased by 35%.
- **Customer Experience Metrics:** Trust scores saw a 42% boost, retention increased by 38%, engagement rate grew by 45%, and resolution accuracy reached 92%.

Building Trust Through Customer Service in the AI Age

"We're also seeing increases in agent productivity—94%—and faster issue resolution at 92%," Kim noted. "The system is reducing agent effort by 87%, which is a change our team appreciates."

Eric Thomas, Chief Strategy Officer, suggested fine-tuning specific areas, like the customer handoff process, to ensure they align with Borenstein's GUARDIAN Digital Trust Framework's™ authenticity principle.

Marcella closed the session by sharing the team's vision for the future. "Our goal isn't to replace human interaction but to enhance it, finding a balance between automation and the personal touch. Customers are optimistic, with over 52% believing AI will improve their experience."

The team was committed to staying at the forefront of AI-driven customer service. "Success lies in transparent, reliable, and personalized interactions," Marcella said, "because trust, once built, must be nurtured at every step."

Borenstein's GUARDIAN Digital Trust Framework™ was more than a strategy—it was a promise to keep human values at the heart of technology-driven transformation. In the coming months, the team will continue integrating AI, keeping transparency, accountability, and trust as the foundation of their customer experience journey.

Marcella closed the meeting, reminding the team, "Trust isn't built in a day. It's built into every interaction, every response, every moment. Let's keep that momentum."

As they filed out, Jake glanced at Kim. "Looks like we're all in the trenches together."

Kim grinned. "Trenches? Try a battlefield. Let's just hope we're winning."

Craft Your Leadership Trust Strategy

Eric drew three interconnected circles. "Here's our AI customer service trust strategy," he began.

Build Trust (Offensive Plays)

"First, we establish service credibility," he explained:

- AI-human collaboration programs
- Service transparency initiatives.
- Customer empowerment systems

Protect Trust (Defensive Plays)

Moving to the second circle:

- Service quality monitoring.
- AI bias prevention
- Customer satisfaction tracking

Building Trust Through Customer Service in the AI Age

Measure Trust

For the final circle:

Trust Metric	Current	Target
Service Trust	70%	95%
AI Satisfaction	65%	90%
Response Quality	72%	85%

"Remember," Eric concluded, "AI-powered service must enhance, not replace, the human touch."

Steps For the Strategic Leader to Build Trust Through Customer Service:

1. **Develop a Centralized Knowledge Base:** Ensure all service agents can access consistent, up-to-date information, reducing errors and confusion.
2. **Implement AI for Speed and Efficiency:** Deploy AI chatbots to manage simple requests, freeing human agents for more complex issues. Speed builds trust.

3. **Continuous Training is Key:** Invest in ongoing training for your customer service team to keep them informed and empowered and ensure they can handle inquiries confidently.
4. **Monitor Financial Investment**: Balance the cost of improvements with the expected return on customer retention and satisfaction.

14. How Brands Can Balance Authenticity and Storytelling to Gain Trust

"The stories we tell literally make the world. If you want to change the world, you need to change your story."

- Michael Margolis

Max had spent the weekend deep in conversation with an old marketing buddy at a tech conference on *Authentic Marketing in the Digital Marketplace*. They'd dissected every trend and tactic, and Max couldn't stop thinking about it. By Monday morning, he was buzzing with ideas.

He called an impromptu brainstorming session with the team. Eric and Kim were the first on board, but he also looped in Jake. The issue? Rezilify's brand narrative—and how it was missing the connection customers craved.

Max started the meeting with his usual enthusiasm. "Alright, team, let's talk authenticity. How do we stop sounding like a corporate robot and start connecting with people on a human level?"

Jake raised an eyebrow. "A human level? Max, we're a cybersecurity company, not a lifestyle brand. People don't need us to be their bestie. They need us to keep their data safe."

Eric, always the contrarian, smirked. "Yeah, I'm with Jake. What's next, heartwarming Instagram posts about firewalls? Maybe a quick clip of Kim walking down the hall, sharing her day and how comfortable her shoes are as she heads to her next HR meeting?"

Max rolled his eyes. "It's not about fluff. It's about trust. We've built a solid reputation on technical reliability, but customers aren't feeling a deeper connection to us as a brand. They trust our products, but they don't *feel* connected to who we are. That's a gap we need to close."

Kim nodded thoughtfully. "I've been watching some of our Glassdoor reviews. Internally, people appreciate transparency and authenticity more than just efficiency. Maybe that's what we're missing externally, too."

Max leaned forward, his energy building. "Exactly! I was talking to a fellow marketer this weekend, and he said something that stuck with me—people don't just buy what you sell; they buy *why* you sell it. The 'why' behind our brand needs to be more real, more relatable."

Eric folded his arms. "Okay, so how do we 'get real'? What do we tell customers about our bad days and tech hiccups? Start an online journal? Share stories like *The Office*? I'm sorry, but it seems a little off base if you ask me." He leaned back in his seat. "But we do need a different approach, so I'm listening."

How Brands Can Balance Authenticity and Storytelling to Gain Trust

Max didn't miss a beat. "That's not as far off as you think. Look at Patagonia or Airbnb. They've embraced imperfection in their messaging, sharing stories that show both their wins and their struggles. People don't expect perfection—they want honesty."

Jake leaned back too, skepticism still on his face. "And how do we pull that off without looking incompetent?"

Max clicked through a few slides, bringing up examples from the weekend's conference. "Take Airbnb. When they rebranded in 2024, they didn't just share glowing stories of happy guests. They let hosts talk about challenges, the difficult parts of hosting, and how they overcame them. The transparency built trust and increased their loyalty by 20%. We can do the same."

Kim, inspired, offered her idea, "What if we start by sharing stories from our own team? We've had challenges. Do you remember the beta test disaster last year? We learned some big lessons from that, and I think that's the honesty customers would relate to."

Max nodded. "I like it. We don't need to pretend everything's perfect. Authenticity is about showing the process, the human side of our company."

Eric rubbed his chin. "So, we make the narrative more about people—our team and our customers—rather than just focusing on our product?"

"Exactly," Max said, energized. "We shift from corporate messaging to a more human-driven story.

We can even involve customers and let them share their real experiences—good or bad."

Jake groaned. "Bad? And we're okay with that?"

Eric chuckled. "It's not about hiding the negatives. It's about showing how we respond to them. Customers want to know we're listening, not just marketing to them."

"OK, I get that," replied Jake, with some understanding.

Max clicked on another slide. "Here's what I'm thinking: three strategies. First, we build an *authentic storytelling* campaign. We share our internal stories—real ones, not polished PR nonsense. Second, we create a *customer-led storytelling platform*, letting them share their experiences directly. Third, we implement *authenticity monitoring* so we can track how this shift is impacting trust and engagement."

Eric stepped in, backing Max's plan. "This can't just be a one-off. We need to measure the impact, fine-tune it, and adapt as we go. That's where Jake comes in."

Jake sighed. "Let me guess—I'm supposed to track all this authenticity in numbers?"

Max smiled. "Pretty much. Sentiment analysis tools, customer feedback, engagement metrics. We'll need all of that to make sure this strategy is actually working."

Kim added, "It's a balance, Jake. Authenticity doesn't mean we lose our professionalism. It's about building trust by being real. Customers appreciate that more than we give them credit for."

Eric looked at the whiteboard, where Max had written out the three strategies. He took the marker to break it down further. "Okay, so we tell real stories, let customers do the same, and monitor it. But if this flops, I'm not taking the blame."

Craft Your Leadership Trust Strategy

Eric drew three interconnected circles. "Here's our authenticity-storytelling trust strategy," he began.

Build Trust (Offensive Plays)

"First, we establish authentic credibility," he explained:

- Story authenticity programs
- Transparency initiatives
- Customer validation systems

Protect Trust (Defensive Plays)

Moving to the second circle:

- Story verification protocols
- Authenticity monitoring
- Trust protection measures

Measure Trust

For the final circle:

Trust Metric	Current	Target
Story Authenticity	70%	95%
Customer Trust	75%	90%
Brand Credibility	68%	85%

"Remember," Eric concluded, "authentic storytelling builds lasting trust."

Steps For the Strategic Leader to Balance Authenticity and Storytelling:

1. **Embrace Authentic Storytelling**: Share stories from within your organization that highlight both successes and challenges. Show the human side of your company and allow employees to be part of your brand narrative.
2. **Encourage Customer-Led Stories**: Create platforms where customers can share their experiences with your product or service.

How Brands Can Balance Authenticity and Storytelling to Gain Trust

Authentic customer stories build trust and strengthen emotional connections.

3. **Monitor Authenticity and Adjust:** Use sentiment analysis and customer feedback tools to measure the impact of your authenticity strategy. Track engagement and make real-time adjustments to ensure your messaging resonates.

Authenticity isn't about being perfect—it's about being real. Building trust with your audience starts by letting them see the human side of your brand.

15. Communicating Brand Values to Gen-Z: Navigating the Authenticity Imperative

"In the age of information, ignorance is a choice."

— Donny Miller

Max stared intently at the screen, a wave of new Gen Z-focused data flooding his mind as he skimmed the latest consumer behavior report from 2024. A knock at his door pulled him back to reality. Eric leaned in, arms crossed, and said, "Max, have you seen the latest engagement metrics with Gen Z?" He stepped further in, eyes narrowing with concern. "We're missing the mark, and it's making us look … well, corporate."

Max gestured for Eric to come in. "Funny you should say that," he said, turning the screen so Eric could see it. "According to this, 85% of Gen Z actively research a company's values before buying, and 76% will switch brands if there's even a hint of misalignment. And now, they're not shy about broadcasting their discontent—almost 8 out of 10 Gen Z consumers will drop us instantly if they sense anything inauthentic. Just *poof*." Max gave a sarcastic wave and smirked.

Eric nodded as he settled into a chair. "And they don't just move on; they tell their networks about it. Gen Z expects brands to take a stand, be transparent, and mean what they say. If there's a perceived gap between words and actions, and the company doesn't respond immediately, they're gone—and they're taking their peers with them."

Max tilted the screen further for Eric. "Look at this. The report shows that 92% of Gen Z trust influencers over traditional brands. That's a seismic shift from just a few years ago. If we're going to reach them, we need to change the game."

"Well," Eric leaned back, arms crossed, "our last campaign was micro-influencer-based, but we need something deeper, more values-driven. Think about Patagonia or Ben & Jerry's—they're more than just brands; they're movements. We're a data security company; why not position transparency and data privacy as our ethical backbone?"

Max nodded thoughtfully. "It has to be genuine, though. Let's commit to more than just marketing buzz. We'll center on transparency and data privacy as our true north. Something that resonates beyond the tagline."

He spun his chair toward the whiteboard and jotted, *"Winning Back Gen Z: Value-Driven Engagement."* Max continued, "Here's what we need: an authentic, robust implementation plan. This generation prioritizes authenticity over polish. We need to show them we mean what we say."

"Definitely," Eric agreed. "A Social Media Engagement Framework, if you will."

Max and Eric brainstormed how to effectively connect with Gen Z on their most trusted platforms, focusing on content that speaks directly to their preferences and values:

TikTok: Short, unfiltered stories that showcase real employees talking about company initiatives and values. Data from 2024 indicates that 93% of Gen Z prefer content that feels raw and honest over highly produced videos.

Instagram: Behind-the-scenes reels highlighting the real people behind the brand. Case studies like those from Nike and Patagonia reveal that showcasing genuine company culture can boost engagement rates by 30%.

YouTube: In-depth, long-form videos featuring panel discussions with experts about the importance of data privacy and transparency.

BeReal: Daily snapshots that show authentic moments within the company, emphasizing transparency and relatability.

Threads (2024 trend): Quick updates, opinion polls, and direct engagement with followers about data ethics, reinforcing an ongoing dialogue.

Key Gen-Z Preferences and Statistics

- **Video Content:** A staggering 95% of Gen Z say video is their preferred way of consuming information.
- **Real-Time Engagement**: Over 88% expect brands to respond to their messages and comments within 2 hours.
- **User-Generated Content (UGC):** Companies that successfully integrate UGC see a 20% higher conversion rate among Gen Z.

Case Study: Duolingo and the Power of Personification

Duolingo's playful approach to branding proved to be a masterclass in engaging Gen Z. By personifying their mascot, Duo the owl, and crafting lighthearted, authentic content around it, Duolingo struck a chord with younger audiences. Over a six-month period, this approach led to a 45% increase in Gen Z engagement, demonstrating the power of relatable storytelling.

"Duolingo didn't just create a mascot," Marcella explained, pulling up Duo's social media posts. "They gave it a personality, one that's cheeky and self-aware, reflecting the humor and style Gen Z appreciates. Through Duo, Duolingo was able to communicate in a way that felt genuine and approachable."

But it wasn't just humor that kept users engaged. Duolingo maintained transparency, sharing both successes and setbacks in its language-learning journey, all in Duo's relatable voice. This combination of authenticity and playfulness broke down barriers, showing that even a brand focused on education could resonate deeply by connecting with users on a personal level.

    Max nodded. "They made language learning feel less intimidating. Duo's personality reminded users that learning can be fun, even when it's challenging."

Implementation Strategy: Authenticity and Value Communication

1. Raw, Real-Time Content

Employee-led storytelling is key. Highlight real experiences and challenges employees face in upholding data security. "We need their voices, not ours, to communicate our values," Eric emphasized.

2. Visualize Our Impact

Develop a public-facing data privacy dashboard that showcases real-time updates on how Rezilify is protecting user data, akin to Spotify's sustainability reports that detail their environmental impact.

3. Employee Advocacy Program

Launch an initiative that encourages employees to share personal stories related to company values. In 2024, brands that used employee advocacy reported a 40% higher trust score among Gen Z audiences.

4. Collaborate with Value-Driven Influencers

Seek out micro-influencers who are known for their commitment to digital ethics and consumer protection. By integrating voices that align with our brand's mission, we gain credibility and reach.

5. Build a Community through UGC

Invite Gen Z customers to share stories about why data privacy matters to them. To reinforce the community aspect, host monthly challenges or AMAs (Ask Me Anything) to engage their participation.

Measuring Success and Key Metrics

Max outlined clear, measurable goals for tracking success:

- **Engagement Rate:** Aim for a 50% increase on TikTok and Instagram.
- **Real-Time Response Rate:** Respond to high-priority interactions within one hour to meet rising expectations.
- **Brand Trust Score:** Reach at least 85% within the first quarter.
- **Alignment with Core Values**: Survey results show 95% recognition rate among audiences about the brand's commitment to transparency.

Craft Your Leadership Trust Strategy

Max drew three interconnected circles on the whiteboard. "Let's map our Gen-Z brand values strategy," she began.

Build Authenticity (Offensive Plays)

"First, we establish genuine connection," he explained:

Core Initiatives

- Value transparency programs
- Social impact campaigns
- Digital storytelling platforms
- Co-creation opportunities
- Purpose-driven content

Protect Authenticity (Defensive Plays)

Moving to the second circle:

Risk Management

- Authenticity monitoring
- Value alignment checks
- Feedback response systems
- Social listening protocols
- Crisis prevention measures

Measure Authenticity

For the final circle:

Metric	Current	Target
Gen-Z Trust	65%	90%
Value Alignment	70%	95%
Digital Engagement	55%	85%
Purpose Impact	60%	90%
Social Resonance	75%	95%

"Let's run a pilot for 60 days," Eric suggested, "and we'll adapt based on what hits and what doesn't."

"Remember," Max concluded, "authentic connection with Gen-Z requires consistent value demonstration, not just a declaration."

* * * *

Weeks later, back in Eric's office, Max and Eric pored over the campaign analytics. Max started, "The transparency initiative led to a 20% increase in brand sentiment among Gen Z."

Eric looked pleased. "And our storytelling strategy? Engagement is up 35%, and our trust rating jumped 25%."

"And those influencer partnerships?" Max continued. "We added 75,000 new followers, and engagement from our target demo skyrocketed. The influencers were genuinely engaged in our mission."

Eric grinned. "We're not just another corporate entity anymore. We're becoming a brand Gen Z trusts because we're speaking their language and walking the talk."

Max nodded. "When we're real, they respond. We're learning how to be a part of their world, not just an interruption in it."

Steps for the Strategic Leader when Targeting Gen-Z:

1. **Launch Platform-Specific, Authentic Content**
   Focus on genuine, employee-driven storytelling that emphasizes transparency and shared values.
2. **Develop a Real-Time Response Strategy**
   Ensure your team is equipped to engage quickly with followers to foster trust and maintain interest.

3. **Create a Data Impact Dashboard**
   Visualize your company's positive contributions to data security and privacy, making complex topics relatable and transparent.
4. **Activate an Employee Advocacy Program**
   Empower employees to share content that aligns with the company's mission. Provide them with training and guidelines but allow personal stories to shine through.
5. **Collaborate with Mission-Driven Influencers**
   Choose influencers who align with your brand's values to create authentic partnerships that resonate with Gen Z audiences.

16. Addressing Security Concerns to Restore Trust in Digital Platforms

"The only way to do great work is to love what you do."

- Steve Jobs

"The latest industry breach report just came in," Jake announced, striding into the executive lounge. "AI-driven cyberattacks are up 225% since last quarter. These aren't just isolated incidents—they're targeting clients through partnerships. We need to act fast."

Eric looked up from his laptop. "Let me guess: advanced phishing and deep fake social engineering?"

"Worse," Jake replied, face grim. "The new wave of AI attacks isn't just about deception; they're exploiting trusted B2B connections to backdoor systems through partner networks. Marcella wants us to regroup now." Jake nodded toward the hallway. "I'm heading up."

Eric closed his laptop with a smirk. "Just got the summons, too. Let's go."

Urgent Meeting: Addressing B2B AI-Driven Security Threats.

Addressing Security Concerns to Restore Trust in Digital Platforms

The team assembled in the sleek, glass-walled conference room under a palpable sense of urgency. Marcella stood at the head of the table, her expression severe.

"This could be catastrophic," Marcella began, gesturing to a slide. "If we don't take immediate, visible action, we'll lose client trust and face serious business impacts." She nodded to Jake, who launched into the specifics.

"AI-enhanced attacks are surging, and the statistics are sobering. Threat actors are using advanced machine learning to bypass traditional security measures, with AI-enabled phishing up 160% and deepfake voice fraud targeting B2B payments up 310%. But what's even more alarming? They're accessing our systems via our partners' networks—exploiting our supply chain to reach us through trusted connections. Our clients' concerns aren't unfounded; these threats are real."

Marcella nodded, adding, "With recent breaches across the tech industry, clients are becoming highly attuned to security lapses. As of 2024, almost 78% of B2B buyers say they prioritize security as a top criterion, and after the Slack breach earlier this year, that figure is only expected to rise."

Max furrowed his brow. "So, what's causing the spike? I thought we were on top of security measures."

"High-profile attacks and the rise of AI mean attackers have tools that bypass many traditional defenses," Marcella explained. "Clients now expect comprehensive, proactive security. This isn't just about compliance—it's about active threat management."

Jake sighed. "What's the budget for all this? We're already stretched."

Eric interjected, leaning forward. "Jake, this isn't just about budget. Security is the cornerstone of trust. If we lose that, we're losing far more than revenue; we're risking the entire business."

Marcella nodded in agreement. "Exactly. Let's focus on solutions to rebuild and secure trust, starting now."

Emerging Threats in 2024: Key Focus Areas

- **AI-Enhanced Attack Vectors**:
    - Automated vulnerability exploitation: up 42%
    - Machine learning-powered phishing: up 160%
    - Deepfake-based B2B fraud: up 310%
    - Supply chain infiltration via partner networks: up 89%

- **B2B-Specific Concerns:**
    - Vendor and partner risk management
    - API and integration security
    - Data segregation across multi-tenant platforms
    - Advanced cross-organization access controls

Addressing Security Concerns to Restore Trust in Digital Platforms

Proactive Security Strategy

Marcella clicked on a new slide. "We need a multilayered approach, addressing both internal and external vulnerabilities, to restore and build client trust. Let's look at specific, actionable measures."

1. Comprehensive Third-Party Security Audit

- *Objective*: Identify and rectify vulnerabilities within our infrastructure, particularly those affecting B2B interfaces.
- *Key Tactic:* Engage a specialized cybersecurity firm with expertise in AI threats to conduct a full audit. We'll implement a 45-day turnaround to detect weaknesses, including those in partner APIs and access points.

"Jake, this falls under your team. Make this a priority so we can show clients concrete proof of our vigilance."

2. Advanced AI Detection & Encryption Protocols

- *Objective:* Use predictive AI to detect threats and anomalies in real time across our B2B interfaces.
- *Key Tactic:* Deploy machine learning models that detect and alert us to high-risk behaviors or irregular access patterns, reinforcing existing protocols.

"Eric, work with our data science team to integrate these protocols and introduce a data encryption layer that's not only compliant, but also adaptive to emerging threats."

3. Client-Facing Real-Time Security Dashboard

- *Objective:* Increase transparency and client confidence by giving clients a live view of security threats and our responsive actions.
- *Key Tactic:* Develop a dashboard that displays active threats, steps taken to mitigate them, and critical metrics, mirroring Google's real-time security reporting.

"Max, coordinate with the client success and dev teams to roll this out within the next 60 days."

4. Partner & Vendor API Security Tightening

- *Objective:* Fortify the security of our APIs and enforce stringent controls for data shared with partners.
- *Key Tactic*: Secure data flows between us and partner networks by using API security tools that offer access control, rate limiting, and anomaly detection.

"Eric, create a roadmap to tighten API connections, including implementing token-based access restrictions and encryption for data exchanges."

5. Enhanced Access Control for B2B Clients

- *Objective:* Provide clients with more control and visibility over their data and system access points.
- *Key Tactic:* Implement multi-level access controls and role-based permissions across B2B interfaces.

"Jake, please add this to the security dashboard so that clients can see and manage their access policies directly."

Measuring Success: Key Metrics

Marcella laid out measurable goals:

- **Client Confidence Metric:** Target an improvement of 25% in client trust metrics within the next quarter.
- **Incident Response Time:** Aim to reduce detection-to-response time by 50% through the real-time dashboard.
- **Data Privacy Complaints:** The goal is to achieve a 20% decrease by implementing enhanced encryption and access controls.
- **API Security Violations:** Achieve a 0% breach rate via upgraded API monitoring and controls.

Implementation Steps and Timeline

Immediate Action Plan:

- Jake: Initiate a comprehensive, third-party security audit focusing on AI-driven vulnerabilities.
- Eric: Strengthen encryption and access control protocols, especially for inter-organizational data exchanges.
- Max: Develop and deploy the real-time client-facing security dashboard.

Craft Your Leadership Trust Strategy

Marcella drew three interconnected circles on the whiteboard. "Let's map our digital security trust strategy," she began. "And the numbers I am giving you are notional benchmarks; you can change them as needed," she added.

Build Security (Offensive Plays)

"First, we establish security credibility," she explained:

Core Initiatives
- Zero-trust architecture
- Data encryption protocols
- Privacy-first frameworks
- Security certifications
- Threat detection systems

Addressing Security Concerns to Restore Trust in Digital Platforms

Protect Security (Defensive Plays)

Moving to the second circle:

Risk Management
- Breach prevention protocols
- Real-time monitoring
- Incident response plans
- Vulnerability assessments
- Compliance auditing

Measure Security

For the final circle:

Security Metric	Current	Target
Platform Trust	72%	95%
Security Score	85/100	98/100
Response Time	15min	5min
Uptime	99.9%	99.99%
Compliance	90%	100%

"Remember," Marcella concluded, "security trust requires constant vigilance and transparent protection measures."

Weeks later, the team reconvened to assess their progress.

Jake started with a sense of relief. "The security audit identified and fixed multiple weak points, particularly in our partner integrations. We've already seen a 20% improvement in client confidence."

Eric added, "We rolled out new encryption and access controls. Clients have more control over their data, and privacy complaints are down by 25%."

Max shared an update on the dashboard. "Clients can now monitor security activity live, which has increased their trust by 15%. The feedback has been overwhelmingly positive; they appreciate the transparency."

Marcella concluded, "We've turned a potential disaster into an opportunity to reinforce client trust. By staying proactive, we're not only addressing threats—we're setting a new standard in cybersecurity for our clients."

The team relaxed, proud of their success. They had turned a crisis into a strength, cementing their commitment to trust and transparency in the eyes of their client.

Addressing Security Concerns to Restore Trust in Digital Platforms

Steps For the Strategic Leader when Addressing Security Concerns:

1. **Conduct a Security Audit:** Hire a third-party firm to assess your platform's vulnerabilities and develop a comprehensive report.
2. **Enhance Data Encryption:** Implement stronger encryption protocols and features that empower users to control their data privacy.
3. **Develop Transparency Tools:** Create client-facing dashboards to allow real-time monitoring of security threats and mitigation efforts.
4. **Communicate Proactively:** Keep clients informed about your security measures and updates, demonstrating that you prioritize their trust and safety.
5. **Build a Culture of Security:** Foster an internal culture that emphasizes the importance of security and transparency at every level of the organization.

17. Overcoming Trust Challenges in B2B and B2C Marketing

"To succeed in business, to reach the top, an organization must be a leader in its field, innovative in its approach, and responsive to its clients."

— Patricia Fripp

Max sat alone in his office, the faint hum of the building's air conditioning the only sound as he mulled over a recent call with a high-profile B2B client. The feedback he'd received was a wake-up call—clients were increasingly frustrated, feeling like their needs were lost in a generic, B2C-style approach. Max sighed, jotting down a few notes just as Eric, Kim, and Jake entered, each with a look of anticipation and readiness.

"Thanks for meeting, everyone," Max began as they sat down. "We've been getting consistent feedback from B2B clients who feel like they're being treated just like consumers. They want tailored solutions and high-touch service, and right now, they're not getting it."

Eric frowned as he settled into his seat. "What kind of specifics are they looking for?"

Overcoming Trust Challenges in B2B and B2C Marketing

Max shook his head. "Customization, personalized insights, and strategic partnership. These clients are paying for premium services, and they're starting to question if they're getting their money's worth."

Kim leaned in, arms crossed. "And for good reason. They're expecting a high-touch, consultative experience and feeling like they're just another account in the system."

Jake, always focused on the numbers, opened a folder he'd brought. "I pulled some recent data. We're facing a 32% trust deficit with our B2B clients, and it's impacting revenue retention by about 18%. There's no question it's time to take action."

Eric looked thoughtful as he reviewed the report. "This is part of a bigger trend. I've seen recent studies showing that 67% of B2B decision-makers say they're more skeptical of vendors than ever. If we don't address this proactively, we're going to lose ground."

Max nodded. "So, how do we rebuild trust? I'm thinking we take cues from some recent case studies."

Eric brought up examples of companies that successfully regained trust in similar situations. "Last year, Microsoft had a cloud outage that tanked trust among enterprise clients. They responded with a real-time status dashboard that gave clients visibility into system health and issue resolution. Within 90 days, their trust metrics improved by 78%."

He continued, "Salesforce launched a 'Trust First' initiative with regular, third-party audits and open transparency reports. Their trust score went up by 52% after six months. Transparency and consistent communication are key."

Max considered this. "It sounds like the framework we need is a structured, transparent strategy that we can sustain long-term. Let's pull from the GUARDIAN Framework to structure our approach."

GUARDIAN Framework for B2B Trust Rebuilding

As they pulled up the GUARDIAN Framework on the screen, Marcella began outlining each component and its relevance for their B2B strategy:

G - Growth Through Authenticity

Marcella started, "Our B2B clients need to feel that we're not only interested in the revenue they bring in but genuinely committed to their growth. By being transparent in how we handle data, prioritize security, and tailor our services to each client's goals, we can demonstrate authenticity. B2B clients should see us as invested partners, not just providers."

U - User Experience Excellence

Max added, "B2B clients want a seamless, intuitive experience in every interaction. We need to simplify their access to reports, insights, and real-time support. If we build easy-to-navigate, customized dashboards and ensure our support team is prompt and proactive, clients will feel that we prioritize their experience every step of the way."

Overcoming Trust Challenges in B2B and B2C Marketing

A - Audience-Centric Analytics

Eric continued, "Our B2B clients each operate in different verticals with unique needs. If we gather and analyze data that's specifically relevant to their industries—like seasonal trends, market shifts, or competitive benchmarks—we can provide insights that are highly relevant to them, showing we truly understand their space."

R - Reputation Management

Marcella added, "Trust takes years to build and moments to lose. Proactively communicating with our B2B clients during any disruptions, owning up to mistakes, and sharing exactly how we're working to resolve issues will strengthen our reputation. We should aim for full transparency in all client interactions, showing we're accountable and communicative."

D - Digital Brand Authority

Max suggested, "Establishing ourselves as experts in our field requires consistent thought leadership with our B2B clients. Publishing industry reports, hosting webinars, and sharing case studies spotlighting our successes will reinforce our authority. When clients see us leading the conversation in digital security and trust while freely communicating that, they'll feel more confident partnering with us."

Don't Believe the Hype

I - Innovative Customer Engagement

Eric said, "Clients want to feel actively engaged, not just managed. We can schedule regular check-ins to update them on new offerings, technology improvements, and best practices they could benefit from. By staying one step ahead and anticipating their needs, we'll show that we're not only listening but constantly innovating on their behalf."

A - Adaptive Marketing Intelligence

Marcella proposed, "Each B2B client's needs and goals are dynamic, so our approach should be, as well. By using adaptive analytics that adjust based on current market conditions and individual client data, we can provide targeted solutions and continually fine-tune our offerings. This level of adaptability will prove we're committed to their evolving success."

N - Network Effect Amplification

Max concluded, "Our B2B clients value community and a sense of shared success. Highlighting other B2B success stories—where clients similar to them have achieved strong results—can reinforce trust in our solutions. Creating forums or networking events for our B2B clients can also help build a network effect, making them feel part of a thriving, supportive community."

This GUARDIAN-driven strategy would enable Rezilify to rebuild B2B trust by focusing on authenticity, tailored experiences, proactive engagement, and continuous improvement—all key elements in fostering long-term relationships with their clients.

Implementation Timeline

"This is going to be a long timeline, folks," Marcella said to the team. Let's take our time and do it properly."

"Yeah," smirked Eric, "Don't want to scare them off or anything."

Months 1-2: Laying the Foundation

- **Growth Through Authenticity**

    o *Weeks 1-2:* Conduct a comprehensive audit of existing client data handling and security practices to identify transparency opportunities.
    o *Weeks 3-4:* Develop clear communication materials that outline how data is handled and protected, highlighting security measures in onboarding documents.
    o *End of Month 2*: Share a "Transparency Report" with clients, emphasizing the ethical and security measures that Rezilify follows.

- **User Experience Excellence**

    o *Weeks 1-2:* Map out the ideal B2B client journey, identifying key

touchpoints where ease and efficiency can be improved.
- *Weeks 3-4:* Build a centralized client dashboard for real-time access to insights, reports, and support channels.
- *End of Month 2:* Launch a beta version of the dashboard with a small client group for feedback.

Months 3-4: Building Engagement and Analytics

- **Audience-Centric Analytics**
  - *Weeks 1-2:* Identify data sources (client data, industry trends) and create a process for gathering analytics tailored to each client's industry and goals.
  - *Weeks 3-4:* Roll out industry-specific monthly reports using pilot groups to test their relevance and value.
  - *End of Month 4:* Regularly distribute personalized insights to all clients based on the analytics collected.

- **Reputation Management**
  - *Weeks 1-2:* Develop a "Trust and Transparency" communication plan, including protocols for proactive updates and clear action plans during disruptions.
  - *Weeks 3-4:* Train client-facing teams on communicating transparently,

owning issues, and proactively sharing updates.
- *End of Month 4:* Launch proactive monthly updates from Rezilify, including service improvements and any identified issues being addressed.

Month 5: Establishing Authority and Adaptive Intelligence

- **Digital Brand Authority**
  - *Weeks 1-2:* Begin developing thought leadership content, such as white papers and case studies, relevant to B2B security trends and solutions.
  - *Weeks 3-4:* Host an initial webinar on the importance of digital trust in cybersecurity, featuring insights from Rezilify's team.
  - *End of Month 5:* Publish thought leadership pieces across various platforms and share these resources with clients.

- **Adaptive Marketing Intelligence**
  - *Weeks 1-2:* Implement adaptive analytics that adjust to real-time client feedback and changing market conditions.
  - *Weeks 3-4:* Integrate adaptive tools within the client dashboard to provide personalized recommendations based on industry-specific trends.

- *End of Month 5:* Start monthly performance reviews with each client, using adaptive data to recommend solutions and strategies.

Month 6: Building Community and Long-Term Relationships

- **Innovative Customer Engagement**

    - *Weeks 1-2:* Schedule quarterly check-ins for each client to discuss their goals, new offerings, and Rezilify's recent developments.
    - *Weeks 3-4:* Develop engagement materials, such as newsletters or webinars, that proactively inform clients of new technologies or best practices.
    - *End of Month 6:* Launch a client-exclusive webinar series highlighting emerging trends, industry insights, and product updates.

- **Network Effect Amplification**

    - *Weeks 1-2:* Identify top client success stories to feature in a "Client Success Spotlight" within newsletters or the dashboard.
    - *Weeks 3-4*: Organize a virtual roundtable for clients to share experiences, successes, and feedback with the Rezilify team.

o *End of Month 6:* Create a community platform or forum where clients can network, exchange insights, and strengthen their connection to Rezilify.

Metrics for Success

1. **Trust Score Improvement:** Aim for a 45% increase in trust scores among B2B clients within six months.
2. **Client Retention Increase:** Target a 38% boost in retention rates by enhancing service and transparency.
3. **Response Time Reduction**: Reduce average issue resolution times by 65% to demonstrate improved responsiveness.
4. **Partner Satisfaction:** Increase client satisfaction score to 82% through proactive, solution-oriented service.

Craft Your Leadership Trust Strategy

Marcella drew three interconnected circles on the whiteboard. "Let's map our B2B and B2C trust strategy," she began.

Build Trust (Offensive Plays)

"First, we establish credibility across markets," she explained:

Core Initiatives

- Case study validation programs

- Client reference networks
- Industry certification systems
- Content authority building
- Thought leadership campaigns

Protect Trust (Defensive Plays)

Moving to the second circle:

Risk Management

- Reputation Monitoring
- Client satisfaction tracking
- Performance verification
- Compliance auditing
- Crisis prevention protocols

Overcoming Trust Challenges in B2B and B2C Marketing

Measure Trust

For the final circle:

Trust Metric	B2B Current	B2C Current	Target
Brand Trust	75%	65%	95%
Client Retention	80%	70%	90%
Satisfaction Score	82%	78%	95%
Reference Rate	65%	55%	85%
Market Credibility	78%	72%	90%

"Remember," Marcella concluded, "trust building requires different approaches for B2B and B2C, but authenticity remains constant across both."

* * * *

The group reconvened 90 days later to review their progress. Marcella joined them, eager for updates.

"Kim, let's start with account management. How's the initial feedback?" Marcella asked.

Kim smiled. "Our clients are responding well. We've already seen a 20% increase in positive feedback, and retention rates have improved by 15%."

Eric said, "Our new marketing campaigns are resonating—emphasizing partnership and tailored service has led to a 20% uptick in qualified leads from targeted industries."

Max looked up from his report. "We conducted an audit on upsell and cross-sell potential and implemented strategies that increased revenue by 10%. Clients appreciate the consultative approach, and it's strengthening our relationships. Using the GUARDIAN Framework has made it so much easier to navigate, and our clients are noticing. "

Marcella nodded approvingly, her expression resolute. "This is what we stand for—proactive, transparent service that prioritizes client success. We're not only rebuilding trust; we're setting a new standard for our B2B relationships. Let's keep this momentum going."

Steps For the Strategic Leader when Building Trust with B2B Clients:

1. **Assess Client Feedback:** Regularly gather and analyze feedback from your B2B clients to identify areas for improvement.
2. **Assign Dedicated Account Managers:** Create a strategy for assigning dedicated account managers to your top-tier clients so they can receive personalized support.

3. **Develop Tailored Marketing Campaigns**: Craft marketing content that specifically addresses the unique challenges and goals of your B2B clients.
4. **Conduct Client Audits:** Perform thorough audits of your existing B2B clients to identify cross-selling and upselling opportunities that add value.
5. **Prioritize Long-Term Partnerships:** Foster relationships emphasizing partnership and collaboration, showing clients you are invested in their success.

PART IV: MANAGING TRUST IN CRISIS SITUATIONS

18. Trust in Crisis Management

"In a crisis, the first thing you should do is to get your story straight and tell it quickly..."

— Brian Stelter.

Marcella leaned back in her chair, her eyes sweeping over her team gathered around the conference table. Jake, Kim, Eric, and Max were all seated, yet each radiating a different level of tension or determination. They had weathered enough crises together to appreciate the weight of what was coming, but this time felt different.

Marcella broke the silence with a wry smile. "When we think we've got crisis management down, the game changes. Now, it's not just about responding; it's about anticipating. If you'd told me in 2022 that we'd be discussing AI-led early warning systems, I would've laughed."

Jake's smirk was tempered by frustration. "Exactly. Remember, we spent months refining the Executive Crisis Guide barely 2.5 years ago, only to be back at the drawing board in weeks. All that work and it feels outdated already."

Max chimed in, leaning forward eagerly. "Well, we can't just keep patching things up. Today's clients expect us to see the crisis coming and handle it before it even happens."

Kim nodded, clutching her tablet. "It's not just the external pressure. I just went through this morning's posts—there's already a buzz over last night's influencer backlash on Rezilify. It's spiraling quickly, pulling in all kinds of criticism. If we don't step in fast, the internal impact will be just as bad as the external."

Eric's eyes flicked from Kim to Marcella, assessing. "This has all the markings of a reputation nightmare, but I think we can turn it around—if we act fast and strategically. Marcella, are we bringing the whole GUARDIAN framework to bear on this one?"

"Absolutely," Marcella replied. "But first, I wanted Jake's take on this shift. He's crunching the numbers to support our new preventive measures. Jake, you know how crucial this is, and we'll need the resources to stay proactive."

Jake rubbed his temples and frowned. "So what's changed? We're still dealing with the same crisis elements—data breaches, PR backfires, misinformation campaigns. How's GUARDIAN going to set us apart here?"

Marcella nodded as if expecting the question. "The difference is in timing and transparency. We're not just here to clean up, but to anticipate and prevent. If a crisis does break, we own the narrative from day one. Look at Microsoft's response to their data breach—they didn't wait. They acknowledged it, offered free identity protection, and kept control. That's what we're aiming for."

Max interjected, enthusiasm brightening his face. "And that's what I've been pushing for in our marketing. GUARDIAN principles align with our brand goals—people want authenticity, responsiveness, and to feel like we're a company that cares enough to be ahead of issues."

Eric, ever the strategist, cracked a grin. "So what's the game plan, then? Are we going the full route—social listening, AI alerts, everything?"

Marcella looked at Jake. "Think of Nike's continuous social listening system. Sure, it's pricey, but catching even one crisis early can be worth every penny. The sooner we detect a potential issue, the faster we can act. It'll mean significant upfront costs, Jake, but I'm confident we'll see the ROI."

Jake raised an eyebrow. "Fine, but I'll need clear metrics. Let's track early incident detections, sentiment shifts, and, of course, financial impact. I want to see the numbers proving it's worth it."

Eric leaned forward, eyes bright. "Metrics won't be hard to track if we go all-in. We'll measure success across customer sentiment, media coverage, and employee morale. It's about proving not just to the public but to our team that we've got this under control."

Kim's face softened with relief. "And we can't ignore internal morale. Employees are hearing this buzz, too. If we equip them with the right talking points and show them a strong plan, they'll know we're confidently handling this."

Marcella nodded. "We'll use GUARDIAN as our response roadmap."

G - Growth Through Authenticity

Max raised a hand, leaning into the GUARDIAN Framework. "Let's take that one by one. Growth Through Authenticity first, right? We put out a statement addressing the criticism transparently. Own our growth opportunities. Show clients we're learning from their feedback."

U - User Experience Excellence

Marcella nodded approvingly. "Spot on, Max. Then, for User Experience Excellence, we'll focus on concrete fixes to any pain points our clients have raised. Let's turn critics into collaborators."

A - Audience-Centric Analytics

Jake tapped his pen thoughtfully. "Audience-centric analytics will show us the themes in the criticism so we can address the biggest concerns. We'll monitor posts and customer support data. Is there any insight we can get?"

R - Reputation Management

"Reputation Management will be critical," added Eric. "We need a crisis team responding in real-time to contain misinformation. Employees should also be prepped with talking points. Internal unity is as essential as external clarity."

D - Digital Brand Authority

"Digital Brand Authority is our opportunity to show leadership here," Marcella emphasized. "A message from me, backed by our commitment to transparency. We'll reassert Rezilify's values, giving clients a reason to keep trusting us."

I - Innovative Customer Engagement

Kim spoke up. "And Innovative Customer Engagement? I'll set up an open Q&A, maybe a live forum, where clients can raise questions. If we stay open and transparent, we won't give critics room to dominate the narrative."

A - Adaptive Marketing Intelligence

"Adaptive Marketing Intelligence is key, too," Max added. "We'll monitor sentiment in real time and adjust our message as we go."

N - Network Effect Amplification

"And finally, Network Effect Amplification," Marcella concluded. "Let's ask our loyal clients and advocates to share their positive experiences. Their voices can help balance the narrative."

Eric looked at Marcella, nodding in approval. "Solid. We'll measure effectiveness across customer sentiment, media impact, and employee morale. Kim is working with HR on a morale survey. We need to know our team feels secure."

Kim straightened, a determined expression replacing her earlier worry. "Got it. The GUARDIAN framework will keep us steady, internally and externally."

Max grinned. "Moments like this show us what we're made of. If we do this right, we'll come out stronger."

Craft Your Leadership Trust Strategy

"That's the plan." Marcella drew three interconnected circles on the whiteboard. "Let's map our crisis trust strategy," she began.

Build Resilience (Offensive Plays)

"First, we establish crisis preparedness," she explained:

Core Initiatives

- Crisis simulation programs
- Response team training
- Communication protocols
- Stakeholder mapping
- Early warning systems

Protect Trust (Defensive Plays)

Moving to the second circle:

Risk Management

- Real-time monitoring
- Rapid response protocols
- Media tracking systems

- Stakeholder engagement
- Message consistency checks

Measure Impact

For the final circle:

Crisis Metric	Current	Target
Response Time	2 hrs.	<30 min
Trust Score	75%	95%
Message Reach	65%	90%
Recovery Rate	80%	95%
Brand Stability	70%	90%

"Remember," Marcella concluded, "crisis management success depends on preparation and swift, transparent response."

Marcella paused and looked around the room, a glint of pride in her eyes. "GUARDIAN isn't just a crisis framework—it's our guide to becoming the brand that people trust because we show up, ready and responsive, no matter what comes our way."

The team exchanged glances, a shared sense of purpose settling over them. Together, they would tackle this challenge head-on, proving to their clients, employees, and themselves that Rezilify could handle anything the digital age threw their way.

Steps For the Strategic Leader when Navigating a Crisis:

1. **Establish a Crisis Response Plan:** Create a comprehensive plan outlining steps for rapid response, direct engagement, and long-term fixes for potential crises.
2. **Monitor Social Media:** Set up alerts for brand mentions and swiftly engage with positive and negative feedback to control the narrative.
3. **Train Your Team:** Ensure your team is prepared to handle crises, emphasizing transparency and honesty in communications.
4. **Review Marketing Claims Regularly:** Conduct periodic audits of your marketing language and product capabilities to ensure alignment and prevent misunderstandings.
5. **Engage Employees:** Keep internal communications open and informative to maintain employee morale and trust during external challenges.

19. Crisis of Confidence - How to Rebuild Trust After a Major Product Failure

"Challenges are gifts that force us to search for a new center of gravity. Don't fight them. Just find a new way to stand."

— Oprah Winfrey, Talk show host and media magnate

Eric, Max, and Jake were already in the conference room, responding to an urgent email from Marcella. The tech team's news that morning had been grim: their latest product launch had failed, and they needed an emergency plan to prevent the erosion of the trust Rezilify had been building.

Marcella entered the room, her expression grave. She placed her tablet on the table, its screen filled with customer complaints and negative media coverage. The urgency of the situation was palpable.

"As you are no doubt aware, we have a major product failure on our hands," Marcella began, her tone serious. "Our latest software update caused significant disruptions for several key clients. I know we've had hiccups before, but this is 100x worse. Customers are furious, and the press is already on it."

Max leaned forward, brows furrowed. "How bad is it?"

Marcella brought the projector to life, displaying a cascade of alarming headlines and social media posts. "Rezilify's Latest Update Crashes Key Systems—Customers Left Hanging" blared from a leading tech outlet, while tweets from outraged customers went viral.

Eric sighed heavily. "This is bad. We promised a seamless update, but instead, we've delivered chaos. We're losing trust fast."

Jake glanced at the financial projections. "We're already seeing cancellations and downgrades. If we don't fix this immediately, we're looking at millions in losses—and that's just the financial side. The bigger cost is the damage to our reputation."

Marcella nodded. "We're in a crisis of confidence. It's not just the technical failure; it's the breach of trust. If we don't act decisively, the fallout will be long-lasting."

Eric tapped his pen against the table, his mind racing. "This isn't just about fixing the software. This is about rebuilding trust. If we don't own this mistake, it will stick with us. We need to act quickly and transparently."

Marcella clicked to the next slide, showcasing a case study from Toyota's 2023 product recall. "We need decisive action. When Toyota faced a massive recall, they didn't hide. They took full responsibility, issued a public apology, and offered compensation. It was costly, but it worked. Customers appreciated the honesty, and their reputation rebounded because they handled it with transparency and speed."

She clicked to the next slide. "All is not lost. Some giants have dealt with similar issues, and we can use their experiences to help us figure this out."

Recent Crisis Management Case Studies

Marcella clicked on the next slide, showcasing two high-profile crisis management examples from 2023 and 2024.

OpenAI Leadership Crisis

When OpenAI's leadership faced a sudden shakeup in late 2023, the impact was immediate: their valuation dropped by $20 billion within five days, and enterprise customer confidence fell by 45%. With trust slipping fast, OpenAI took decisive action. The company restructured its board and enhanced governance transparency, openly addressing the concerns of clients and partners. This approach worked; within 60 days, OpenAI had regained 70% of the trust they had lost, stabilizing their position in the market.

Boeing 737 MAX Crisis

In early 2024, Boeing was hit with another crisis related to its 737 MAX series, leading to a staggering $28 billion market value loss. Confidence among airline partners dropped by 52% as safety concerns resurfaced, threatening Boeing's reputation and future orders. In response, Boeing launched a rigorous plan, instituting enhanced safety protocols and committing to transparent, ongoing communication with stakeholders. While recovery has been gradual, Boeing has achieved a 25% improvement in trust levels through these sustained efforts.

Marcella pointed to the GUARDIAN Framework slide. "We can apply the GUARDIAN Framework here," she said, "which emphasizes transparency, accountability, and proactive risk management. When used effectively, this Framework doesn't just manage crises—it can actually enhance trust. It calls for decisive actions on three fronts: owning the issue, implementing structured communication, and adopting preventive measures."

"Of course!" Eric chimed in, with a nod to Kim. "We used the GUARDIAN Framework for that tech-influencer situation recently—it's a solid roadmap. We just need to follow it step-by-step."

Crisis Recovery Framework

Immediate Response Protocol

- Acknowledge within 2 hours
- An initial statement within 4 hours
- Action plan within 24 hours
- Daily updates to stakeholders

Communication Strategy

- Transparent messaging across all channels
- Regular stakeholder updates
- Real-time response to concerns

- Clear accountability statements

Eric nodded as he reviewed the steps. "So, we need to act with speed and integrity. Admit our failure, lay out our plan, and assure our customers that we're implementing preventive measures, so this doesn't happen again."

Marcella looked around the room, gauging the seriousness on their faces. "Exactly. This is a moment where transparency is non-negotiable. If we can't restore trust, we're finished." She stood and began writing on the whiteboard: Ownership, Compensation, Prevention.

Ownership and Apology Strategy

- *Objective:* Take full responsibility for the failure and communicate openly with affected customers.
- *Key Tactic:* Issue a public apology within 24 hours, explaining the issue and outlining the steps to fix it. Acknowledge the disruption and reassure customers that the situation is under control.

"Max, we need a clear, honest statement out by the end of the day. Customers must know we take this seriously and will provide ongoing updates."

Max nodded firmly. "I'll draft it right after this meeting. We'll own the mistake, no excuses."

Customer Compensation Strategy

- *Objective:* Compensate affected customers to rebuild goodwill and show that we value their trust.
- *Key Tactic:* Offer affected clients compensation through service extensions, refunds, or enhanced support. This mirrors Toyota's approach during the recall, which helped it restore customer loyalty.

Marcella turned to Jake. "We can't worry too much about the budget right now. It'll cost us more to win lost customers back than to keep the ones we have happy. Let's offer fair compensation to show we're serious."

Jake leaned forward. "I agree. We need to compensate customers fairly and quickly—whether through refunds or free service extensions. I'll ensure this gets rolled out efficiently."

Marcella nodded, "Ensure all compensation plans are communicated to our customers in 30 days."

Prevention and Future Trust Strategy

- *Objective:* Prevent future failures and restore confidence in our reliability.
- *Key Tactic:* Conduct a full post-mortem on the product failure, identify the root causes, and implement system-wide improvements. Publish a report detailing the changes to reassure customers that this won't happen again.

Marcella looked at Eric. "We need to identify where we went wrong and ensure it doesn't happen again. Customers need to see that we're taking concrete steps to improve."

Eric nodded. "We'll get to the bottom of it and make the necessary changes. Then, we'll be transparent about what we've done."

Craft Your Leadership Trust Strategy

Marcella drew three interconnected circles on the whiteboard. "Let's map our product crisis recovery strategy," she began.

Build Recovery (Offensive Plays)

"First, we establish confidence restoration," she explained:

Core Initiatives

- Immediate response protocols
- Customer compensation programs
- Product improvement systems
- Communication transparency
- Quality assurance overhaul

Protect Trust (Defensive Plays)

Moving to the second circle:

Risk Management

Don't Believe the Hype

- Impact assessment tracking
- Customer feedback loops
- Quality monitoring systems
- Brand sentiment analysis
- Recovery verification

Measure Recovery

For the final circle:

Recovery Metric	Current	Target
Customer Trust	45%	90%
Product Confidence	55%	95%
Brand Sentiment	40%	85%
Quality Score	65%	95%
Recovery Rate	50%	90%

"Remember," Marcella concluded, "rebuilding trust after product failure requires immediate action, complete transparency, and measurable improvement."

* * * *

When the team gathered to assess their progress, Max reported, "The public apology was issued within 24 hours, admitting the failure and reassuring customers that a fix was in progress. The transparency was well-received, and social media sentiment began to shift positively. Ongoing updates kept customers informed, and the anger started to subside."

Marcella smiled. "Good job, Max. Let's keep moving forward with this. Our focus isn't just on survival; it's on emerging stronger with a renewed commitment to our customers."

Steps for the Strategic Leader to Recover from a Product Failure:

1. Own the Mistake: Take immediate responsibility. Issue a public apology that clearly explains the issue and your resolution plan.
2. Communicate Transparently: Provide regular updates to affected customers. Keeping them informed helps restore confidence and shows you care.
3. Offer Fair Compensation: Assess the impact on customers and provide appropriate compensation. Whether through refunds, service extensions, or additional support, ensure customers feel valued.
4. Conduct a Post-Mortem: After addressing the immediate crisis, analyze what went wrong. Identify root causes and implement changes to prevent future issues.
5. Publish Findings: Share your findings and improvements with customers. Transparency about your processes builds trust and demonstrates your commitment to quality.

20. Effective Crisis Management to Rebuild Trust and Win Back Customers

"Failure is simply the opportunity to begin again, this time more intelligently."

- Henry Ford

The tension in the executive lounge was palpable as Jake paced the floor, his frustration obvious after a recent call with one of Rezilify's board members. "This is insane. Speculation is spiraling, and it's about to cost us one of our biggest clients," he muttered, glancing over at Kim and Max. "It's not even the facts—the rumors are killing us."

Kim looked up, concerned. "What exactly did they say? Are there actual complaints, or is it just fear talking?"

Jake shook his head, sighing. "It's all based on speculation around a data breach we contained months ago. Our client knows it was addressed, but they're reacting to the chatter online as if we're hiding a ticking bomb."

Max leaned back in his chair, a cynical smile on his lips. "Remember when Zoom's stock tanked after privacy concerns in 2020? They had to scramble to rebuild trust with encryption updates and a transparency campaign. Speculation alone nearly cost them everything. We're in cybersecurity, though—trust issues hit us twice as hard."

"Exactly," Jake replied, visibly frustrated. "People don't wait for the facts. They assume the worst, and we're left scrambling to fix the narrative."

Kim folded her arms, nodding thoughtfully. "Then we need to act fast and develop a clear, comprehensive strategy—both for clients and the public."

Max leaned forward. "It's like Zoom. They controlled the message by publishing weekly, transparent, specific security updates targeted at calming fears. We need to move just as fast."

Jake considered Max's words, his determination hardening. "We need to stop rumors from snowballing, which means going beyond transparency alone. Clients are already worried; we must give them a reason to stay."

Kim chimed in, "Our response needs layers: proactive communication with clients, consistent internal updates, and tangible client incentives. We can't afford any ambiguity."

Max nodded in agreement. "Let's divide the responsibilities. I'll lead the public-facing side—an immediate statement with weekly client and media updates outlining our security improvements. Transparency will be key here."

Effective Crisis Management to Rebuild Trust and Win Back Customers

Detailed Crisis Recovery Plan with Tech Protocols and Metrics

1. Personal Outreach Program

Objective: Re-establish direct communication with lost clients, demonstrating accountability and authenticity.

Approach:

- Each high-value client receives personal outreach from senior leadership within the first 72 hours.
- Structured one-on-one meetings or calls, allowing clients to express their concerns directly to decision-makers.
- Example: In 2024, Apple handled a similar issue by assigning client managers to personally manage VIP accounts, recovering nearly 70% of affected accounts.

Metrics for Effectiveness:

- Customer Sentiment Analysis: Track changes in sentiment across social platforms and customer feedback channels after outreach.
- Churn Rate Reduction: Measure if outreach decreases churn rates in the following weeks.

2. Customized Recovery Plans

Objective: Tailor solutions to each client's pain points to demonstrate commitment to resolving specific issues.

Approach:

- Build individual client profiles detailing past complaints, product use, and preferred outcomes.
- Assign account managers to personally oversee recovery for each client.
- Example: After a similar PR setback, Google Cloud implemented client-tailored service agreements to address unique client concerns, significantly boosting client retention and satisfaction.

Metrics for Effectiveness:

- Client Retention Rates: Track the percentage of clients who re-engage after receiving tailored recovery solutions.
- Usage Metrics Post-Reengagement: Track usage metrics, such as engagement with newly implemented features, to assess if the recovery solutions resonate with clients.

3. Financial Incentives and Value-Added Services

Objective: Offer tangible, exclusive benefits to clients who consider returning, showcasing both value and loyalty.

Approach:

- Provide special pricing options, such as long-term discounts or bundled services, to

demonstrate commitment to valued relationships.
- Offer additional credits for future purchases, limited-time upgrades, or access to premium support channels.
- Example: After a supply chain disruption, Amazon Web Services implemented loyalty-based pricing, recovering nearly 80% of affected customers and improving long-term retention rates.

Metrics for Effectiveness:

- Return Rate on Incentive Offers: Measure how many clients accept and return after being offered incentives.
- Increase in Customer Lifetime Value (CLV): Track CLV to ensure re-engaged clients remain profitable over the long term.

Trust Recovery Monitoring: Key Metrics and Protocols

1. **Sentiment Analysis Using AI-Based Monitoring Tools**

   - Use AI tools to track real-time customer sentiment and keyword trends related to the crisis and the company's name.
   - Tools such as Brandwatch or Sprinklr can help gauge shifts in public perception daily, allowing immediate response adjustments.

2. **Customer Satisfaction Scores Post-Outreach**

- After each outreach and recovery initiative, survey clients to measure their satisfaction with the company's response and their trust in its future reliability.
- High satisfaction rates post-outreach correlate with trust recovery, while low scores indicate areas needing improvement.

3. **Reduction in Churn Rate and Increased Renewal Rates**

    - Track churn rate before and after recovery initiatives to assess the plan's effectiveness in retaining clients.
    - Renewal rates among previously dissatisfied clients are a strong indicator of regained trust.

4. **New Client Referrals and Positive Reviews**

    - Monitor for increased positive reviews, testimonials, and client referrals after recovery actions. Satisfied clients often provide referrals or leave positive reviews, indicating they feel confident in the company's restored reputation.

Craft Your Leadership Trust Strategy

Jake drew three interconnected circles on the whiteboard. "Let's map our customer recovery strategy," he began.

Build Recovery (Offensive Plays)

"First, we establish customer confidence," he explained:

Core Initiatives

- Customer outreach programs
- Compensation strategies
- Service improvement plans
- Communication campaigns
- Feedback integration systems

Protect Trust (Defensive Plays)

Moving to the second circle:

Risk Management

- Sentiment monitoring
- Recovery verification
- Customer retention tracking
- Feedback analysis
- Crisis prevention protocols

Measure Recovery

For the final circle:

Recovery Metric	Current	Target
Customer Return	55%	90%
Trust Score	60%	95%
Brand Sentiment	50%	85%
Satisfaction Rate	65%	90%
Loyalty Index	45%	85%

"Remember," Jake concluded, "winning back customers requires a genuine commitment to change and transparent communication of improvements."

"I'll handle internal communications," Kim added. "Our employees need to know exactly what's happening to avoid internal rumors. I'll schedule a town hall meeting to address any concerns and reinforce our security commitments directly."

Jake nodded, tapping his fingers on the table. "I'll focus on retention. We can't afford to lose more clients over a rumor. I'll put together a compensation package with extended services for affected clients to show them we're serious about making things right."

Max added, "We need a timeline for all of this. I'll draft the public statement by tonight and start weekly updates immediately. We'll monitor social sentiment daily to track any narrative shifts."

Kim nodded. "Internal communications will go out tomorrow morning, and the town hall will happen by the end of the week. Consistency will be critical for the next few weeks."

"And I'll have the compensation packages ready by week's end," Jake said. "I'll reach out to our most at-risk clients individually. This needs to be personal and immediate."

The three executives exchanged a look of mutual determination. Jake spoke up, "Let's reconvene in a week to see where we stand and adjust as needed."

* * * *

When they gathered again a week later, the tension had eased slightly, but the room was still focused and cautious.

"So, how did we do?" Jake asked, looking at Max and Kim expectantly.

Max smiled as he pulled up some data. "The public statement went out as planned, and social media backlash has dropped by 25% since then. The weekly updates are working—clients are responding positively, and we're regaining control over the narrative."

Kim nodded. "Internally, things are calming down. The town hall was a success. Employees feel more informed and confident, which also helps on the client-facing side."

Jake looked visibly relieved. "Good. We've kept 80% of the at-risk clients on board with the compensation packages. Quick action has paid off."

Max added, "This proves the point: controlling the narrative with transparency, communication, and concrete actions is the only way to counter speculation."

"Let's keep the momentum," Jake said. "We've bought ourselves some time, but this isn't over. We'll check back in two weeks and track any progress."

Steps For the Strategic Leader to Recover from a Crisis:

1. **Act Fast and Own the Narrative**: Address speculation immediately to prevent it from spiraling. A prompt response limits the spread of misinformation.
2. **Communicate Transparently:** Publish consistent updates on your problem-solving efforts to keep stakeholders informed and reassure them.

Effective Crisis Management to Rebuild Trust and Win Back Customers

3. **Offer Proactive Solutions:** Provide clients with incentives or added value that show you're taking their concerns seriously.
4. **Control Internal Messaging**: Ensure employees are informed to prevent internal rumors from destabilizing morale and client trust.

21. Rebuilding Brand Reputation Amidst Internal and External Crisis

"In crisis management, trust is your most valuable currency. Lose it, and the cost is immeasurable,"

- Debbie Millman

Marcella stood at the head of the table in the boardroom, a sense of urgency etched into her usually composed demeanor. She placed a stack of newspapers and magazine clippings down with a thud, her gaze scanning the faces of her team—Eric, Max, Jake, and Kim—each well aware that this meeting was anything but routine.

Marcella passed around the clippings. "We're in a PR storm. And this time, it's not just about our product failure. It's about how we've been handling things internally. Someone leaked our internal discussions, and the media ran with it."

"It gets worse," Kim added, her voice tight. "I've seen the Glassdoor reviews, and my team has been sharing their concerns. This leak didn't just hit the media; it's fueling internal unrest too."

Marcella clicked on the projector, displaying the most damning headline of them all: *"Internal Strife at*

Rebuilding Brand Reputation Amidst Internal and External Strife

Rezilify? Leaked Emails Show Leadership in Disarray."

"We have to face this," Marcella said firmly. "Internal emails showing disagreements among leadership are all over the news, and our customers are starting to wonder if we're falling apart. This isn't just about managing PR anymore. This is personal."

Max shook his head, eyes narrowed as he read the headlines again. "I've been tracking the media coverage. It's brutal, and transparency is key. But we need to make sure we don't fuel the fire."

Eric didn't hold back, his frustration palpable. "The internal issues becoming public shouldn't have happened. But now that they have, we can't ignore them. We need to take control of the narrative, or this will define us."

Jake leaned back, scanning the numbers on his tablet. "Investors are getting jumpy, and clients are worried about our stability. If we don't act fast, this could cost us more than just reputation—we'll start losing business."

Kim nodded in agreement, her voice soft but resolute. "And internally, employees are looking for answers. Retention will become our next crisis if we don't reassure them and address the cultural issues exposed by this leak."

Marcella paced, her mind already calculating the path forward. "Agreed. This crisis is a turning point. We need a structured response, which means following the GUARDIAN Framework closely. Let's use the strategy to turn this around and come out of it stronger."

Strategy Planning: GUARDIAN Framework in Action

Marcella wrote *Transparency, Unity,* and *Reform* on the whiteboard and underlined each term.

"First," she said, "we own up to the mistakes and rebuild transparency. Max, I want you to organize a press conference where we address the leaked emails head-on. We'll explain the disagreements and show that they reflect a team willing to debate tough issues, not one in disarray."

Max nodded, jotting down notes. "I'll get it organized. This can't be about spin—we'll need to emphasize the real changes we're making."

Marcella turned to Eric next. "Unity is our next priority. We're setting up a leadership retreat to realign our vision and strategy. Eric, book it at that fishing lodge on the river—somewhere isolated to talk openly. We'll document our outcomes, and ensure they're communicated to everyone internally and externally."

Eric nodded thoughtfully. "The sooner, the better. I'll set it up for the next two weeks. This will allow us to air our differences and emerge with a unified stance."

Marcella turned to Jake and Kim. "And lastly, reform. Jake, you'll lead on developing a leadership training program focused on conflict resolution and communication. Publicize the progress so that our stakeholders see that we're actively working on improving."

Jake raised an eyebrow, his voice wry. "Got it. No kumbaya, but we'll show we're committed to real change. I'll have a detailed plan ready for you within the week."

Marcella looked at Kim. "We need HR's full support on this. Kim, I want you to ensure the internal messaging reflects our commitment to change. Partner with Jake on the program so that it resonates with employees and addresses the cultural issues exposed by this crisis."

Action Plan: Crisis Management Strategy

With the team assembled, Marcella outlined the GUARDIAN-driven action plan for addressing the crisis and rebuilding trust:

Phase 1: Immediate Crisis Management

1. **Press Conference**—Max will lead a transparent, upfront conference on the leaked emails, emphasizing the strength of their team's openness.
2. **Social Media and Media Engagement** – Eric will ensure consistent, clear messaging in every public-facing communication.
3. **Sentiment Monitoring** – Track daily customer sentiment to assess the immediate response.

Phase 2: Rebuilding Trust Internally and Externally (Days 2-14)

1. **Leadership Retreat** – Eric will organize the retreat, ensuring alignment and unified direction.
2. **Transparent Communication** – Document the outcomes of the retreat and communicate them to employees and clients.

Phase 3: Long-term Recovery (Days 15-45)

1. **Leadership Training Program** – Jake will lead a conflict resolution and communication training program, documenting progress to reinforce a commitment to reform.
2. **Internal Communication Strategy**: Kim will monitor employee sentiment and ensure HR support reflects Rezilify's renewed commitment to cultural improvement.

Craft Your Leadership Trust Strategy

Marcella drew three interconnected circles on the whiteboard. "Let's map our PR crisis recovery strategy," she began.

Build Recovery (Offensive Plays)

"First, we establish narrative control," she explained:

Rebuilding Brand Reputation Amidst Internal and External Strife

Core Initiatives

- Rapid response protocols
- Message alignment systems
- Stakeholder communications
- Media engagement plans
- Story repositioning strategies

Protect Trust (Defensive Plays)

Moving to the second circle:

Risk Management

- Media monitoring
- Narrative tracking
- Sentiment analysis
- Message consistency
- Crisis containment

Measure Impact

For the final circle:

Recovery Metric	Current	Target
Media Sentiment	45%	90%
Story Control	60%	95%
Public Trust	55%	85%
Message Reach	65%	90%
Brand Recovery	50%	95%

"Remember," Marcella concluded, "turning negative headlines positive requires swift action, consistent messaging, and measurable results."

* * * *

Fifteen days in, Max's press conference had gone live. The team had addressed the leaked emails candidly, framing the disagreements as part of a healthy, passionate culture of innovation. The media narrative shifted, highlighting Rezilify's openness to confronting its challenges.

Rebuilding Brand Reputation Amidst Internal and External Strife

Thirty days in, Eric's leadership retreat had successfully realigned the team. Public communication after the retreat reinforced Rezilify's united front, and the messaging resonated with employees internally. Engagement metrics indicated increasing employee confidence, marking a shift from the initial unrest.

By day 45, Jake's leadership training program was well underway, emphasizing conflict resolution and improved communication. The published reports on their progress calmed investors and reassured clients, further bolstering the company's reputation.

Executive Reflection: Turning Crisis into Opportunity

As the team gathered again in Marcella's office, there was a sense of cautious optimism. Max reviewed the media sentiment results. "The press conference made an impact. The media is shifting focus from dysfunction to resilience."

Eric nodded. "And the retreat brought us back together, giving everyone a renewed sense of purpose. Employees notice the change, and our public messaging reflects that unity."

Kim added, "I'm seeing it internally, too. Morale is climbing. Employees are seeing real reform, and it's restoring their confidence."

Jake leaned back, satisfied. "Our training is a work in progress, but it's having an effect. Investors feel reassured, and the structured program keeps clients informed."

Marcella allowed herself a small smile. "We've shown that we can weather a crisis—and come out stronger. But we have to ensure these changes stick."

The team looked around the room, seeing the collective strength that had gotten them through. Rezilify's transformation was underway, with each executive committed to shaping a new narrative defined not by crisis but by resilience, unity, and trust.

Steps for the Strategic Leader to Rebuild Reputation after a PR Crisis:

Own the Narrative: When internal issues spill into the public eye, address them directly. Host a press conference or release a transparent statement that shows leadership is united in solving the crisis. The quicker you control the narrative, the less damage the story will do.

Rebuild Internal Trust: Crises often expose weaknesses in leadership or culture. Use this as an opportunity to realign your leadership team. A focused retreat can help solidify a unified vision, which should be communicated to employees and stakeholders.

Commit to Reform: Don't just pay lip service to change. Implement tangible reforms such as leadership training programs or new communication processes. Publicize these changes to reassure your

Rebuilding Brand Reputation Amidst Internal and External Strife

stakeholders that you're committed to long-term improvement, not just short-term crisis management.

Turning a crisis into an opportunity is possible but requires swift, transparent action, a unified leadership team, and a commitment to real reform.

22. Rebuilding Trust After a Digital Crisis or Scandal

"It takes many good deeds to build a good reputation and only one bad one to lose it."

- Benjamin Franklin

The team gathered at their usual lunch spot, surrounded by the remains of sandwiches and salads. It had been months since Rezilify's product failure and perceived data breach, and while the storm had mostly passed, the long shadow it cast over customer trust lingered.

Marcella, leaning back in her chair, broke the silence. "Alright, team. Good lunch. But let's not kid ourselves; it's time to talk shop. We've made strides since the product failure, perceived breach, and PR scandal, but it still feels like we're paddling against the current."

Max, scrolling through his phone, looked up, "No kidding. I got the trust survey results earlier. We're up about 15% from the lowest point after the PR thing, but we're nowhere near where we need to be. I thought our transparency play would have done more by now."

Jake raised an eyebrow as he jabbed at the last bite of his sandwich. "Fifteen percent? That's not going to impress the board. We're burning cash on trust-building, and it's trickling in. I get it—trust takes time—but at some point, I need numbers to justify this."

Eric, ever the strategist, smirked. "Jake, you always want to plant a seed in the evening and see a tree by morning. Trust doesn't work like that. It's more like—watering a cactus." He chuckled before adding, "This isn't a quick fix; we're in it for the long haul."

Marcella nodded, her face serious. "Exactly. The easy part was the transparency we've shown by using GUARDIAN—addressing the issues openly, issuing regular updates, and getting that security audit going. Now, it's about earning back trust day by day."

Kim, silent until now, put down her iced tea and jumped in. "And it's not just about what we say, but how we say it. People must feel we're genuinely on their side, not just ticking boxes. There's no room for corporate fluff anymore; they can spot that a mile away."

Max looked up from his phone. "Right. We're still in recovery mode. The initial transparency gave us a small win, but the honeymoon phase is over. If we want to regain trust, we need to continue to show them, not tell them, that we're improving. That's what they're waiting for."

Max leaned back, folding his arms. "So, what's next? We've made the statements and done the updates. The audit is in progress, but the needle's barely moving. Do we just wait and hope it turns around?"

Marcella shook her head. "No waiting. We need to stay in front of this. Look at how Johnson & Johnson handled their vaccine concerns. They didn't just issue one apology and go silent—they stayed visible, partnered with authorities, and ensured the message kept getting out there. We need to do the same."

Max perked up. "I agree. We need to keep that drumbeat going. But not just more emails or press releases—we need to focus on actions. Maybe ramp up customer engagement and show them how we lead security innovation. We could gather some real user testimonials to reinforce that we're safer now."

Jake, ever the pragmatist, leaned in. "That's great for optics, but how do we measure it? I need data that shows this campaign is actually moving the needle."

Eric smirked. "Ah, Jake, always with the numbers. We can track customer churn, NPS scores and support ticket trends…all signs of how people feel about us. But trust isn't as quantifiable as the bottom line."

Kim nodded. "He's right, but we can still track sentiment. I've been watching employee morale, too. We've made strides internally—communication's better, and there are fewer complaints on Glassdoor. That'll help, but it needs to align with how we're perceived externally."

Marcella spoke up again, decisive as ever. "Right. And once the audit is done, we don't just release the good stuff. We go public with everything—the fixes we're making, the issues we still need to solve. Transparency is the long game, and we can't avoid the ugly parts."

Eric grinned. "Brutal honesty—the new frontier of corporate PR."

Kim chuckled. "Yeah, but it works. People don't expect us to be perfect; we are just accountable. Trust will follow if we can own up to our mistakes and keep showing progress. It's slow but steady."

Jake sighed. "Okay, I can get behind that. But let's be clear—if we're still crawling after six months, we may need to revisit the budget."

Marcella smirked. "We'll keep an eye on the numbers, Jake. But like Max said, it's about showing up consistently. We've already survived the initial hit—now, we need to show that we've learned and grown from it. When we return to the office, I'll map out a rubric for us to follow."

Kim raised her glass, looking around the table. "Here's to rebuilding trust. One honest conversation at a time."

The team nodded, feeling the weight of the task ahead and a sense of determination.

Craft Your Leadership Trust Strategy

Back in the office, Marcella drew three interconnected circles on the whiteboard. "Let's map our digital crisis recovery strategy," she began.

Build Recovery (Offensive Plays)

"First, we establish digital credibility," she explained:

Core Initiatives

- Digital audit protocols
- Platform security overhaul
- Transparency programs
- Data protection systems
- Crisis response teams

Protect Trust (Defensive Plays)

Moving to the second circle:

Risk Management

- Digital monitoring
- Breach prevention
- Reputation tracking
- Platform security
- Incident response

Measure Recovery

For the final circle:

Recovery Metric	Current	Target
Digital Trust	55%	95%
Platform Security	75%	99%
User Confidence	60%	90%
Data Protection	80%	99%
Recovery Rate	65%	95%

"Remember," Marcella concluded, "rebuilding digital trust requires immediate action, complete transparency, and robust security measures."

Steps for the Strategic Leader to Rebuild Trust:

1. **Consistency in Communication:** Keep customers informed, not just once, but repeatedly. Transparency needs to be maintained long after the initial crisis response.

2. **Show, Don't Just Tell:** Actions speak louder than words. Implement meaningful changes and let customers see the improvements firsthand through testimonials, case studies, and regular updates.

3. **Complete Transparency:** Publish results of audits or investigations, warts and all. Own up to mistakes and communicate the steps being taken to fix them.

4. **Internal Alignment:** Trust-building starts internally. Improve internal communication and ensure employees are aligned with the company's direction, as this will reflect externally.

5. **Measure Sentiment and Results:** Use customer churn, NPS scores, and support ticket trends to gauge how trust is being rebuilt. Track progress and adjust strategies as needed.

6. **Long-Term Commitment:** Trust isn't rebuilt overnight. Keep reinforcing positive messages through authentic actions and consistent communication over time.

23. Crisis of Trust in Data Management

"The truth is rarely pure and never simple."

— Oscar Wilde

Marcella strode into the conference room, frustration clear on her face. "Thanks for dropping everything to meet, everyone," she said, sitting. "We've got a serious trust issue with our data management practices. Customers are starting to doubt how secure their data is with us."

Max, already seated with Eric and Jake, looked surprised. "What? Our protocols are some of the best. We've never had a major breach. Just a few minor incidents we got under control right away."

Eric interjected, "It's not about the breaches, Max. It's about perception. Customers aren't technical; they don't care how good our systems are if they don't trust us to protect their data."

Jake leaned back, mulling over Eric's point. "So, it's back to perception. And once that doubt creeps in, it's hard to shake. Promises won't cut it—we need proof."

"Exactly," Marcella agreed. "And we need to address it now before this erodes further."

Max sighed, "But what more can we do? Our systems are rock solid. What if customers are just being paranoid?"

Eric pulled up a file on his tablet. "Take a look at Equifax from last year. After their data breach, they did everything right on paper—strengthened security, made public apologies, and offered free credit monitoring. But they were too late to be transparent. The public didn't care about their response; they remembered the delay in being informed. They never regained trust because customers felt misled."

Marcella nodded. "Exactly. Look at how Apple tackled this in 2024—they proactively launched App Tracking Transparency, putting privacy control in users' hands before it became an issue. Customers trusted them because they acted before being forced."

Max sighed, rubbing his temples. "Alright, I get it. But how do we know when customers will get skittish about a non-issue next?"

"That's where we use the GUARDIAN Framework to stay proactive," Marcella explained. "Let's guide them through our data security practices transparently and assure them of control at every step. Max, I want you to lead a proactive transparency campaign around data protection—think of it as our modern 'Executive Guide' but customer-facing. Let's show our customers exactly how we handle their data and offer them control."

Max sat up, ideas forming. "We can frame it around giving customers visibility and control. I'll have my team design a public dashboard with clear data on our security metrics and management practices. We'll get this live in 30 days."

"Perfect," Marcella agreed. "And no corporate jargon—our customers need to feel like we're lifting the curtain."

Jake added, "We must back this up with solid evidence, too. I'll lead an internal audit of our data protocols and publish a transparency report. We'll show the details of our security practices and any areas we're improving—no more waiting until something goes wrong."

Eric chimed in, "Good call, but let's be careful. Not everyone understands cybersecurity jargon. I'll manage the educational content, making it digestible for our customers. We'll explain exactly what our data practices mean and why they matter."

Marcella smiled with a mix of relief and determination. "Perfect. We need this to be as clear as Microsoft's AI ethics campaign last year. They made complex topics like AI bias understandable to everyone. We need that same level of clarity for our data practices."

Max summarized, "So, I'll handle transparency, Jake's got the audit and report, and Eric will cover education. If we execute this right, customers will feel reassured, in control, and in the loop."

"Exactly," Marcella said with a hint of pride. "Let's get to work."

Craft Your Leadership Trust Strategy

Eric drew three interconnected circles. "Here's our data management trust strategy," he began.

Build Trust (Offensive Plays)

"First, we establish data credibility," he explained:

- Data transparency programs
- Quality verification systems
- Stakeholder communication protocols[1]

Protect Trust (Defensive Plays)

Moving to the second circle:

- Data monitoring systems
- Privacy protection measures
- Breach prevention protocols

Crisis of Trust in Data Management

Measure Trust

For the final circle:

Trust Metric	Current	Target
Data Trust	25%	90%
Privacy Score	70%	95%
Quality Rating	68%	85%

"Remember," Eric concluded, "data trust requires quality and transparency."

* * * *

When Marcella gathered the team for an update, she was eager to see the results of their efforts. "Alright, let's see where we're at."

Max shared his screen, showing the data transparency dashboard. "The campaign launched on time, and initial feedback's been fantastic. We've seen a 15% increase in customer confidence. People are responding positively—they appreciate the insight into our practices."

Jake followed. "The audit is complete, and we published the transparency report. No major vulnerabilities surfaced, and 20% of customers cited the report as a reason they trust us more."

Marcella turned to Eric. "And the education piece?"

Eric nodded. "Educational content went live last week. Engagement is up 10% among customers who want to learn more about our practices. They're seeing the value in what we do, not just hearing our promises."

Marcella leaned back, visibly satisfied. "This is exactly what we needed. We've turned perception around by being transparent, educating our customers, and taking real action. But let's remember—trust isn't a one-and-done deal. We've set the foundation, but we must keep proving ourselves daily."

Eric agreed, "Trust is ongoing. But with this approach, we're finally ahead of the curve."

Max smirked. "Lesson learned—if we're proactive, we stay ahead of the rumors and keep control of the narrative."

Jake added, "And we've got the proof to back it up. Transparency, education, and real action—that's our new formula for trust."

Steps for the Strategic Leader to Build Trust in Data Management:

Proactive Transparency: Get ahead of potential trust issues by being open about your data management practices. Apple's App Tracking Transparency initiative empowers customers by giving them control and visibility into how their data is handled before concerns arise. Don't wait for a crisis—make transparency an ongoing practice.

Conduct and Publicize Audits: Regular internal audits should be a core part of your strategy, but it's not enough to do the audit. Publish the results in a transparency report, ensuring customers see tangible proof that your systems are secure. Demonstrating accountability builds credibility and reinforces trust.

Educate Your Customers: Don't assume your customers fully understand data security. Break down your practices in clear, accessible terms to make complex issues easy to understand. Use educational content to demystify your processes and help customers see the value in your data security efforts.

Tailor Communication for Clarity: Avoid vague jargon. Whether publishing transparency reports or educating customers, ensure your communication is simple, clear, and jargon-free. Customers need to understand what's happening behind the scenes and why it matters to them.

Build Trust with Tangible Actions: Transparency must be backed by evidence such as audit results and security improvements. Ensure that measurable actions support every promise. Consistent updates and visible results will maintain and strengthen customer confidence over time.

Monitor Feedback and Adjust: Track customer sentiment closely to measure the impact of your transparency initiatives. Use feedback to refine your approach and continue building trust. As seen with the 15% increase in customer confidence in the campaign, these efforts should have tangible results that can guide future decisions.

Commit to Continuous Improvement: Trust-building isn't a one-time effort. It requires sustained attention and constant reinforcement. Regularly revisit your data management and transparency strategies, and continue evolving to meet customer expectations in an ever-changing digital landscape.

PART V: LEVERAGING TRUST FOR GROWTH

24. Corporate Social Responsibility (CSR) and Brand Purpose in Trust Building

"A brand for a company is like a reputation for a person. You earn a reputation by trying to do hard things well."

— Jeff Bezos, Founder and executive chairman of Amazon

This month's strategy meeting in the Rezilify boardroom started late, as Marcella had been on a call with the Board. She bustled in and stood at the head of the table.

"Alright, team," she said, her voice cutting through the chatter. "We've got a growing concern from our customer base, especially the younger demographic. They're calling us out for a lack of visible corporate social responsibility efforts. In the age of transparency, clients expect us to stand for something more than just profit."

Max leaned forward, nodding. "I've seen the numbers. More than 80% of Millennials report being more loyal to companies aligning with their values. Despite our efforts last quarter, I imagine we're falling behind."

Corporate Social Responsibility (CSR) and Brand Purpose in Trust Building

Jake smirked as he always did when these kinds of topics came up. "So, what do they want now? For us to save the planet, too? We're a cybersecurity firm, not Greenpeace."

Eric shot him a glance. "It's not about saving the planet, Jake. It's about showing we care. Whether it's environmental impact, ethical business practices, or community involvement—our customers want to know we're not just in it for the bottom line."

Kim joined in, her voice steady. "Exactly. The ripple effect is that our employees want to be proud of where they work, too, and that starts with transparency around this. Showing them we're committed to social responsibility will also improve our internal culture."

Marcella nodded, hands on her hips. "We need to effectively communicate what we're already doing. We're committed to more than just cybersecurity; we're committed to ethical practices and community engagement."

Marcella clicked the projector remote, and a slide flashed with a stark headline: "Lack of CSR Visibility = Loss of Trust Among Key Demographics." She turned to the team. "Let's revisit this trust by the generation thing. This is the heart of the issue." She paused. "Millennials and Gen Z, in particular, are values-driven. They care about more than what we offer and why we do it. Right now, there's a disconnect between our messaging and our mission."

Max pulled out his tablet and tapped the screen. "Look at Unilever. Their Sustainable Living Plan helped them connect with socially conscious consumers, leading to a 50% increase in trust among Millennials in 2023. Their products with purpose-driven messaging grew 69% faster than the rest of their portfolio."

Eric added, "And don't forget Patagonia—they're the poster child for embedding social responsibility into a brand's DNA. They pledged 1% of their sales to environmental causes. It's not just talk; it's part of who they are. They've turned that into a massive trust-building tool."

Jake leaned back, grinning sarcastically. "Right, so we need to be more like Patagonia? It's easy for them; their brand is about saving the planet. Ours is about stopping hackers."

Marcella shot him a sideways look. "We don't need to reinvent ourselves, Jake. We need to clarify our core values. Data privacy and security are ethical issues. We're already protecting people's most sensitive information; we just need to communicate how that contributes to a bigger picture."

Kim interjected, "Let's not forget the importance of our internal culture. Engaging employees in these expanded initiatives will boost morale and create advocates for our brand."

Marcella returned to the whiteboard and began jotting down key points for the team to tackle.

Corporate Social Responsibility (CSR) and Brand Purpose in Trust Building

CSR Communication Strategy

Objective: Communicate Rezilify's ongoing efforts on ethical data practices and cybersecurity, positioning it as a socially responsible brand.
Key Tactic: Launch a content campaign highlighting our work's social and ethical impact, much like Unilever's Sustainable Living campaign.

"It is imperative that we get this right. Max, I'm assigning it to you and your team."

Max leaned back in his chair, nodding. "We'll show our clients how our commitment to data privacy and security isn't just about business—it's about doing what's right. We're already protecting them; we must tell that story better."

Community Engagement Program

Objective: Engage with local communities through partnerships and volunteer programs that align with Rezilify's values.
Key Tactic: Develop a program where employees can volunteer at cybersecurity awareness workshops, similar to Salesforce's employee engagement initiatives.

Marcella looked at Eric. "This could be the best way to reach our customers. I'm assigning this to you, Eric."

Eric nodded. "We'll get our team involved in the community. Cybersecurity is a public issue, and we can show we care about protecting everyday people, not just corporations."

Sustainability Commitment

Objective: Incorporate sustainable practices into Rezilify's operations to appeal to environmentally conscious consumers.
Key Tactic: Implement a sustainability initiative focused on reducing energy consumption in data centers inspired by Microsoft's environmental goals.

Marcella turned to Jake with a wry smile. "I need you to see what we can do on this side. I know you may think it seems a bit futile, but it's important we check for possible ways to tweak or reduce Rezilify's footprint."

Jake sighed. "Fine, I'll look into it. We're already using a lot of energy running those servers, but I'll crunch the numbers and see where we can cut back."

"Good," Marcella smiled at the team. "We'll reconvene in three months to discuss what we found."

Craft Your Leadership Trust Strategy

Marcella drew three interconnected circles on the whiteboard. "Let's map our CSR and brand purpose strategy for building trust," she began.

Build Purpose (Offensive Plays)

"First, we establish authentic social impact," she explained:

Corporate Social Responsibility (CSR) and Brand Purpose in Trust Building

Strategic Initiatives

- Environmental sustainability programs
- Community engagement initiatives
- Employee volunteer opportunities
- Ethical sourcing guidelines
- Social impact partnerships

Protect Purpose (Defensive Plays)

Moving to the second circle:

Risk Management
- ESG compliance monitoring
- Impact verification systems
- Stakeholder feedback loops
- Third-party audits
- Transparency reporting

Measure Purpose

For the final circle:

Impact Area	Current	Target
ESG Score	75/100	95/100
Community Impact	65%	90%
Employee Engagement	70%	95%
Carbon Footprint	-20%	-50%
Social ROI	2.5x	4x

"Remember," Marcella concluded, "authentic social responsibility builds lasting trust when it aligns with our core values and demonstrates measurable impact."

* * * *

The team gathered in the same room to review the progress of their CSR initiatives.

As usual, Max went first, excited to share his progress. "The CSR communication campaign launched on time, and early results are strong. We've

Corporate Social Responsibility (CSR) and Brand Purpose in Trust Building

seen a 15% increase in consumer trust, especially among Millennials. They're engaging more with our content, and we're getting positive feedback on our positioning."

Eric added, "The community engagement program has been a hit, too. We've already run cybersecurity awareness workshops in two local schools, with three more scheduled this quarter. Not only did it excite our employees, but we also got great press coverage, boosting employee engagement by 10%."

Jake, still skeptical but impressed, shared his part. "I ran the numbers. We've significantly reduced energy consumption, especially by optimizing our data centers. We've cut operating costs by 5% and improved our standing with environmentally conscious customers." he paused as a smug grin crept across his face. "Not bad for a cybersecurity company."

Kim smiled, clearly pleased. "That's kind of a big deal. It's important to recognize how this work enhances our overall company culture and makes us a more attractive employer."

Marcella smiled, satisfied. "We've shown that we're not just about protecting data—we also care about making a positive impact. And our customers are noticing."

As the team started to wrap up, Marcella paused, looking around the room. "We've made real progress here. Good work, team." She took a deep breath and acknowledged the moment. "But the work doesn't stop. CSR isn't just a campaign; it's something we need to weave into everything we do."

Max nodded in agreement. "We've been talking the talk. Now, we need to keep walking the walk."

Eric leaned back, looking thoughtful. "It's funny—we've been doing the right thing all along; we just weren't telling anyone. Now that we are, people are seeing us differently."

Jake raised his eyebrow. "Maybe there's hope for Rezilify saving the planet after all," he joked, but there was a glint of respect in his eyes.

Marcella laughed, shaking her head. "It's not just about saving the planet, Jake. It's also about saving people's trust in us to do the right thing. And right now, we're doing both."

With that, the team left the boardroom feeling more aligned than ever. Rezilify wasn't just a cybersecurity company anymore—it was a company with a purpose, and that made a significant difference.

Steps for the Strategic Leader for Developing CSR and Brand Purpose:

1. **Assess Current Initiatives**: Review your company's existing CSR efforts and identify areas for improvement or better communication.

2. **Engage Employees:** Involve your employees in CSR initiatives to foster a sense of pride and advocacy for your brand.

3. **Develop a Communication Strategy**: Create a campaign highlighting your business practices' ethical and social impact.

4. **Community Involvement:** Establish partnerships with local organizations and encourage employee participation in community service.

5. **Sustainability Goals**: Set measurable targets for reducing your company's environmental impact and communicate these goals transparently to stakeholders.

25. Building Trust Through Strategic Innovation

"The art of progress is to preserve order amid change and to preserve change amid order."

- Alfred North Whitehead, Mathematician and Philosopher

The office buzzed with activity, quiet energy filling the halls as Rezilify's latest win rippled through the team. Eric leaned against the counter at the water cooler, sipping his coffee. Beside him, Jake's usual calm demeanor held a hint of satisfaction.

They were relaxed—a rare moment, given the pressure of the past months. But this success was well-earned. The results were quick, confirming they were on the right track and providing the necessary validation.

"Are we congratulating ourselves?" Max grinned, approaching with his trademark energy. "Because we should."

Eric glanced at Jake, smirking. "Well, we finally cracked it, didn't we?"

Jake nodded. "I still can't believe we pulled it off without burning through the budget." He crossed his arms, looking pleased. "Balancing innovation and trust isn't easy."

Max laughed. "You're telling me! We spent months figuring out how to innovate without losing the faith of our customers—or Marcella's, for that matter." He paused, his expression shifting to something more thoughtful. "But, you know, our approach this time was different. We listened."

Jake chuckled. "Yeah, Max. For once, you and your team didn't push out twenty flashy features in a month."

Eric grinned. "And that's what made the difference. We weren't just throwing things at the wall to see what stuck. We took a page out of the Apple playbook on privacy. Remember their 2023 rollout? They didn't just react; they showed leadership by making privacy a core feature. We applied that thinking here."

Max leaned in, his enthusiasm clear. "Exactly. Instead of launching every new idea, we zeroed in on what mattered to our users. Marcella pushed us on this—customer-centric innovation, she called it. My team spent 60 days diving into feedback and their pain points."

Jake sipped his coffee, nodding. "And the ROI showed up quickly. At first, I wasn't thrilled with the budget hit for that kind of research, but the results spoke for themselves. We focused on two key areas—security and ease of use—and saw a 25% bump in customer satisfaction."

Eric raised an eyebrow, his sarcasm briefly absent. "The real impact wasn't just from what we built but how we communicated it. Customers needed to know we weren't innovating just to compete; they needed to see us solving their problems."

Max grinned. "That's where your team came in, Eric. The messaging overhaul wasn't just some slick marketing trick. We told customers: 'Here's how we're addressing the issues you told us about.'"

Eric nodded, a hint of pride creeping into his voice. "We shifted the conversation. It's like what Amazon does. Their messaging always starts with the customer, and we followed suit. We saw a 15% rise in trust because customers could finally see us as proactive leaders, not just responders. And that trust? It showed up in the numbers. Retention rates improved."

Max's eyes gleamed with satisfaction. "And that phased rollout, Jake? Total game-changer."

Jake chuckled, clearly pleased. "Yup. We controlled the rollout, starting with a beta group of our most loyal users. Their feedback helped us refine the features before the full launch. We didn't dump everything on customers all at once like we used to."

Eric smirked. "Yeah, that was a bit chaotic, looking back."

Jake continued, "This time, it worked perfectly. We gathered real feedback, made a few tweaks, and when we rolled it out, it was seamless. Churn dropped by 12%, and those early adopters felt like we were paying attention."

Max crossed his arms, his smile widening. "The results say it all. Customers trust us because we didn't just move fast—we moved smartly. Now, we're not just keeping up; we're ahead."

Craft Your Leadership Trust Strategy:

Later that day, Marcella gathered the team in the conference room, ready to cement the lessons from their success into a trust-driven innovation strategy. She drew three interconnected circles on the whiteboard.

"Let's map our digital innovation trust strategy," she began. "This isn't just about celebrating a win. We need to build a playbook for the future."

Build Trust (Offensive Plays)

"First, we establish innovation credibility," she explained:

- Digital innovation programs
- Customer-centric development
- Technology trust protocols

Protect Trust (Defensive Plays)

Moving to the second circle:

- Innovation risk assessment
- Technology safety measures
- Customer protection systems

Measure Trust

For the final circle:

Trust Metric	Current	Target
Innovation Trust	70%	90%
Technology Safety	75%	95%
Customer Confidence	68%	85%

"Regularly review these metrics to keep us accountable," Marcella emphasized. "Innovation must enhance trust, not erode it. These numbers will show us where we stand."

With the strategy set, Marcella looked around the room, a satisfied smile crossing her face. "Great work, everyone. Let's keep this momentum going."

As the meeting concluded, the team felt the satisfaction of a job well done and the reassurance of a roadmap for future wins. Each leader walked away with a renewed commitment to balancing innovation with trust—a balance that, at Rezilify, was now a cornerstone of success.

Steps for the Strategic Leader to Build Trust through Strategic Innovation:

Customer-Centric Innovation: Focus on addressing customers' real needs, not just chasing trends. Start with comprehensive feedback sessions to identify the most impactful issues, then design solutions around them.

Clear, Purposeful Messaging: Communicate why each innovation matters. Show customers that your updates solve their problems and aren't just features to match competitors.

Phased Rollouts: Introduce new features gradually, starting with a beta group. Collect early feedback to adjust and ensure a smooth user experience upon full launch.

Measure Trust Impact: Track satisfaction and churn rates to assess whether innovations strengthen or strain customer trust.

26. Building Trust Through Transparent Innovation and Social Proof

"The key to building trust through technology is designing solutions prioritizing user empowerment, privacy, and transparency."

— Tim Berners-Lee

Marcella studied Rezilify's latest AI-powered marketing dashboard, where real-time analytics highlighted a 32% increase in customer trust scores. With numbers like these, she knew her executive team needed to understand the powerful effect of transparent technology on their customer relationships and overall trust. She called them to discuss how this shift was reshaping marketing and how Rezilify connected with its clients at every stage.

"Here's what we're seeing," Marcella began, displaying their latest campaign results on the screen. "When we're transparent about using AI in marketing, customer engagement increases by 45%. But it's not just about acknowledging AI; it's about showing how it enhances the human experience."

Max, always ready with an idea, nodded enthusiastically. "Look at our content strategy. Since we began tagging blog posts with 'Enhanced by AI, Curated by Humans,' authenticity ratings have

Building Trust Through Transparent Innovation and Social Proof

jumped 28%. Customers appreciate knowing the balance of tech and human insight."

Eric chimed in with an industry case study. "Sephora's a great example. They increased customer engagement by 74% last quarter by being upfront about their AI-driven personalization. They turned AI from a hidden tool into a trust-building feature."

"And then there's Starbucks," Max added. "Their Deep Brew AI program helped transform their loyalty program. By explaining how AI personalizes recommendations, they've boosted customer satisfaction by 40%."

Marcella summarized their approach, emphasizing the importance of visibility and ethics in tech adoption. "The future of marketing isn't about hiding AI," she said. "It's about showcasing how it can deepen customer connections."

As the team gathered in the meeting room, Marcella sketched three interconnected circles on the whiteboard: Build Trust, Protect Trust, Measure Trust.

Craft Your Leadership Trust Strategy

"Here's our AI ethics trust strategy," she began.

Build Trust (Offensive Plays)

"First, we establish AI ethics credibility," she explained:

- AI transparency programs
- Ethics governance initiatives
- Stakeholder engagement systems

Protect Trust (Defensive Plays)

Moving to the second circle:

- AI bias monitoring protocols
- Ethics compliance verification
- Algorithm auditing measures

Building Trust Through Transparent Innovation and Social Proof

Measure Trust

For the final circle:

Trust Metric	Current	Target
AI Ethics Trust	70%	95%
Algorithm Transparency	75%	98%
Stakeholder Confidence	68%	85%

"Remember," Marcella concluded, "ethical AI builds lasting trust through transparency and accountability."

* * * *

A couple of weeks later, Kim and Max grabbed a coffee from a vendor's cart outside their office, eager to review the impact of their latest social proof initiatives.

"Max, did you see the reports?" Kim asked, her excitement clear. "Our testimonial library has transformed the sales team's conversations. They're able to counter objections with real client success stories."

Max grinned. "Absolutely. We've given the team a set of conversation 'cheat codes.' Social proof is huge in B2B—especially for companies trying to minimize risk. But we can go even deeper to build trust across the customer journey."

Kim was intrigued. "Where do you suggest we start? We have a huge opportunity to emphasize social proof, not just as a way to overcome objections but to build confidence from the first interaction."

Max thought for a moment. "Let's tackle the awareness phase first. Prospects researching us are looking for credibility—peer recommendations, partnerships, case studies. Adding verified client logos to our website and LinkedIn pages will create instant confidence."

Kim nodded, jotting down notes. "Recognizable brands signal trust. It's the 'if *they* trust Rezilify, I can, too' mentality. And during the evaluation stage?"

"We need testimonials that address specific pain points—like onboarding ease, measurable ROI, and support quality," Max replied. "Imagine pairing each FAQ with a client quote or video addressing that question."

Kim's eyes lit up. "Perfect! We also should add employee endorsements on Glassdoor and LinkedIn. Clients appreciate seeing a committed, happy team; they know if employees are satisfied, the company is solid."

Max nodded, impressed. "Employee voices add a layer of authenticity you can't replicate in polished

Building Trust Through Transparent Innovation and Social Proof

marketing pieces. We could highlight employee satisfaction metrics on social media, showing clients we prioritize quality for both our team and clients."

Kim leaned forward. "What about during the purchase phase? This is when trust is crucial."

Max's excitement grew. "How about client reference calls? Set up short chats between current clients and prospects—nothing builds trust like hearing it from a peer. Adobe did this with their AI suite last year and saw a big increase in close rates."

Kim jotted this down, nodding. "And we could add short testimonials in sales proposals. Just before clients sign, they see real-world examples of the ROI they can expect."

Max nodded. "And post-sale is where the real trust-building happens. Imagine sending new clients a welcome video featuring another client's success story—instantly building a sense of community."

Kim smiled, raising her coffee cup. "This kind of social proof makes B2B partnerships feel personal and impactful."

"You bet," agreed Max, "can't wait to see what everyone else saw too."

They entered the conference room and relayed what they saw from the initiative.

Content Marketing Evolution

Max leaned forward. "Our blog readership has grown by 65% since we started explaining how AI refines our content. We're not just publishing articles; we're showing customers how tech helps us serve them better."

Social Media Authenticity

Eric added, "Our social listening tools detect sentiment with 92% accuracy, but the real value comes in how we share that with customers. Every AI-powered interaction is labeled, and trust scores rise steadily."

Email Marketing Innovation

Max continued, "Personalization is key. Our AI-driven email campaigns hit 85% relevance ratings by transparently explaining how we use customer data to create a better experience."

Marcella smiled as she concluded, "In 2024, marketing success isn't just about what technology we use. It's about how we use it to foster genuine connections."

27. Key Ways B2B Companies Can Use Testimonials to Overcome Objections

"People trust people, not companies."

– Debbie Millman.

The leadership team found themselves at their go-to lunch spot, an upscale café with a sprawling view of the city skyline. The informal setting made for the best brainstorming sessions, but today's vibe was a bit urgent.

Marcella didn't waste time as she picked up her fork. "We need to talk about B2B sales objections—specifically the trust issues we face. We keep hearing the same thing: 'Can we trust Rezilify to deliver?'"

Max smirked, swirling his iced tea. "Our product is rock solid. Why the hesitation?"

Marcella sighed, clearly frustrated. "It's not about the product, Max. It's about trust. B2B clients are skeptics by nature. They need proof that we've succeeded in their shoes."

Jake leaned back and crossed his arms. "So what's the magic bullet? Hit them with financials? You know how much I love a good spreadsheet."

Eric shot him a sarcastic grin. "Oh yeah, nothing screams 'trustworthy' like rows of numbers. No, Jake, what we need is social proof. Testimonials. People in their industry who've faced the same doubts and came out winning with us."

Jake raised an eyebrow. "So we're outsourcing B2B selling now?"

Max chuckled, rolling his eyes. "Exactly. As we saw with Gen-Z, B2B clients trust their peers more than they trust us. Testimonials are gold in this game. If we can show companies like them that others have faced the same concerns and succeeded, we'll knock down those objections."

Kim finally jumped in, having been listening quietly. "It's not just about testimonials. It's about what I call 'social truth'—authentic stories from real customers that reflect our genuine impact. In B2B, trust doesn't just come from case studies. It comes from social credibility—Glassdoor reviews, LinkedIn endorsements, even the way our team talks about our successes online."

Eric nodded in agreement. "Exactly. It's like how we've leveraged LinkedIn for recruitment. Companies in the B2B space are watching every move we make on social platforms. We should highlight those testimonials across all our social touchpoints—creating a stream of trust that runs deeper than a sales pitch."

Kim leaned forward, her tone serious. "And let's not forget internal trust. If our employees don't believe in the message we're selling, how can we expect our clients to? We need to integrate this internally, too. Make sure our teams feel confident and proud of our work, so they're naturally talking about it on their platforms."

Marcella nodded. "So, social truth both externally and internally. I like it. But let's keep the sales process simple. Eric, what's the strategy?"

Eric didn't miss a beat. "Take a page from Salesforce's 2024 Executive Guide. They didn't just share random quotes—they aligned specific testimonials with specific objections. Were they worried about ROI? Show the success story of a client who saved 25%. Skeptical about the ease of integration? Here's a client who rolled out the same product in half the time they expected. Adobe did the same in 2023 with their AI suite—targeted, verifiable success stories."

Jake, still chewing his sandwich, grinned. "So, we let other people do the heavy lifting."

Max nodded enthusiastically. "Exactly. Social proof is ten times more effective than anything we can say ourselves. And Kim's right—we need to broadcast this social truth in sales decks, across social media, in our recruitment, and even internally."

Kim added, "It's all about authenticity. Prospects and employees alike need to see that our success isn't just something we say—it's something they can believe."

Craft Your Leadership Trust Strategy

Eric turned his tablet to show the table and drew three interconnected circles. "Here's our B2B testimonial trust blueprint," he began.

Build Trust (Offensive Plays)

"First, we establish testimonial credibility," he explained:

- Client success verification
- Industry-specific testimonials
- Case study development

Protect Trust (Defensive Plays)

Moving to the second circle:

- Testimonial authenticity checks
- Client relationship monitoring
- Success story verification

Key Ways B2B Companies Can Use Testimonials to Overcome Objections

Measure Trust

For the final circle:

Trust Metric	Current	Target
Testimonial Impact	70%	90%
Client Trust	75%	95%
Conversion Rate	68%	85%

"Remember," Eric concluded, "authentic testimonials are your strongest trust signals."

Marcella tapped her fork on the table, thoughtful. "Alright, let's give the sales team an arsenal of real stories to handle every objection. We also need to ensure those stories are everywhere in the world—on social media and review sites. I want clients to see proof before they even talk to us."

"I'll have my assistant email the Action Plan once we return to the office."

Action Plan: Social Proof and Testimonial Strategy

1. **Testimonial Library for Sales Teams**

   - *Objective:* Use targeted testimonials to address common objections in the B2B sales process.
   - *Action:* Build a library of testimonials organized by specific objections, such as ROI, cost, implementation, and ease of use. Leverage real stories from clients to tackle the biggest pain points head-on.
   - *Assigned to*: Max Jordan (CMO)
   - *Deadline:* 30 days.
   - *Expected Result:* A 25% increase in sales effectiveness when handling objections.

2. **Video Testimonials for Social Truth**

   - *Objective:* Boost credibility with authentic video testimonials from clients who've faced similar challenges.
   - *Action:* Create a series of short video testimonials showing real clients explaining how Rezilify solved their problems. Spread these across social media, LinkedIn, and internal communication to reinforce authenticity.
   - *Assigned to:* Eric Thomas (CSO) and Kim Rogan (CHRO)
   - *Deadline:* 45 days.

- *Expected Result:* A 20% boost in trust metrics during sales.

3. **Testimonial Integration in Sales Presentations**

    - *Objective*: Build credibility by weaving testimonials into sales pitches.
    - *Action:* Develop sales presentations that directly integrate relevant testimonials addressing specific client concerns, ensuring that prospects see proof of success from similar industries.
    - *Assigned to:* Jake Benjamin (CFO)
    - *Deadline:* 30 days.
    - *Expected Result:* A 15% reduction in the sales cycle.

4. **Social Media Amplification of Testimonials**

    - *Objective:* Leverage social media to boost external trust.
    - *Action:* Broadcast client success stories on LinkedIn, Twitter, and other platforms to amplify B2B social truth. Encourage employees to share testimonials organically through their channels.
    - *Assigned to:* Max Jordan (CMO) and Kim Rogan (CHRO)
    - *Deadline:* Ongoing.
    - *Expected Result:* A 30% increase in engagement and client trust online.

* * * *

A few weeks later, at an industry lunch, the conversation turned to the results they had seen on the strategy to use social proof and B2B testimonials to build trust with new clients.

Max was the first to speak, grinning as he put down his drink. "The testimonial library is live, and it's killing it. Our sales teams love it—clients are responding to the success stories, and we've already seen a 25% bump in overcoming objections."

Kim agreed, "Early reports are favorable, and our customer-facing teams love having verified proof of success with existing clients to share when new clients express doubt."

Eric followed up. "The video testimonials are a hit. Prospects love seeing real faces talk about real outcomes. Trust metrics have shot up by 20%."

Jake nodded. "The presentations with testimonials built-in have shortened the sales cycle by 15%. People trust what they see, especially when it's someone in their situation."

Kim smiled, satisfied. "We've built trust not only with our clients but also within our team. Our employees are more engaged, sharing these stories themselves—proof that social truth works both ways."

Marcella leaned back, pleased. "We've shown them proof. Now they believe us. That's how we keep winning."

Steps For the Strategic Leader to Build Trust with Testimonials:

1. **Leverage Social Proof:** Build a library of targeted testimonials to address specific objections in the sales process.

2. **Use Video for Authenticity:** Video testimonials offer an engaging and trustworthy way to show real client success.

3. **Integrate Testimonials in Sales Decks**: Tailor presentations to feature relevant testimonials based on client pain points.

4. **Amplify Social Truth:** Use social media to broadcast success stories and encourage employees to share organically to reinforce trust internally and externally.

PART VI: CULTIVATING TRUST WITHIN THE ORGANIZATION

28. Building a Culture of Trust Within the Organization

"Trust is the glue of life. It's the most essential ingredient in effective communication. It's the foundational principle that holds all relationships."

— Stephen Covey

Kim Rogan (CHRO) entered Jake Benjamin's office, closing the door behind her. Unlike their usual meetings focused on financial projections, this one carried a more sensitive weight—trust, or the growing lack of it, within their own company. "Thanks for making some time, Jake."

Jake, busy scrolling through spreadsheets, glanced up. "What's the urgency, Kim?"

Kim sighed, dropping into the chair opposite him. "It's not external this time, Jake. It's internal. We've spent so much energy rebuilding customer trust that we've lost sight of what's happening here with our people."

Jake paused, his brow furrowing. "You mean morale?"

"Not just morale," Kim said, her tone sharpening. "Trust. Our latest employee survey shows a significant drop—over 40% of employees don't trust leadership. I think that constitutes a crisis."

Jake leaned back, folding his arms, defaulting to skepticism. "I knew communication was getting rocky, but trust? That's a bigger issue. What's the cause?"

Kim pulled up the data on her tablet, showing him a breakdown of the survey results. "There are several reasons. Inconsistent communication from leadership, lack of transparency in decision-making, and employees feeling disconnected from the company's direction. We've been adding all the extras to their roles. It's all adding up."

Jake looked at the screen, eyebrows raised. "Damn. That's a morale killer, for sure. But what's the real risk here? Are we talking about high turnover?"

"Yes," Kim replied. "If people don't trust us, they won't stick around. Worse, the ones who stay will disengage. You know as well as I do how that affects productivity and innovation."

"Alright," Jake said, sitting up straighter. "What do we do about it?"

Kim flipped to another slide. "We start by rebuilding from the ground up. Transparency, empowerment, and communication. We need to show our employees we're listening and that we're committed to change."

Jake smirked. "Is this one of those soft HR fixes where we just throw out some inspirational memos?"

Building a Culture of Trust Within the Organization

Kim shot him a playful glare. "If I wanted to do that, I wouldn't be sitting here with you. No, we need a real plan. And we can't do it alone. We're going to need the whole leadership team involved to turn this around."

Jake nodded, sensing the gravity of the situation. "Okay, so what's the plan? And how do we get the others on board?"

"Here's what I'm thinking,"

The Plan: Building a Culture of Trust

1. Transparent Leadership

Action Step:

Objective: Improve transparency and leadership visibility.
Tactic: Launch a monthly Leadership Transparency Forum.
Assigned to: Kim Rogan
Deadline: 30 days.

Kim: "First, we need to be transparent—radically so. I'm proposing a monthly 'Leadership Transparency Forum.' Employees will have direct access to us, where they can ask questions and hear firsthand about key decisions. No hiding behind vague emails."

Jake scratched his chin. "A forum where they can ask anything? That could get messy."

"Exactly," Kim said with a smile. "It'll be tough, but that's the point. If we want to rebuild trust, we need to be open, even if the questions make us uncomfortable."

2. Empower Employees to Be Heard

Action Step:

> *Objective:* Empower employees to actively participate in decision-making.
> *Tactic:* Establish an Employee Trust Council with monthly meetings.
> *Assigned to:* Kim Rogan and Jake Benjamin
> *Deadline:* 30 days.

Kim leaned forward. "We need to give employees a platform to voice their concerns and ideas in a structured way. I think we form an 'Employee Trust Council,' where representatives from each department meet with leadership regularly to discuss issues and opportunities."

Jake raised an eyebrow. "You're putting them at the table with us?"

"Yes," Kim said firmly. "If we want them to trust us, they need to see that their input matters."

3. Consistent, Clear Communication

Action Step:

> *Objective:* Ensure consistent, aligned communication from leadership.
> *Tactic:* Implement leadership communication training.
> *Assigned to:* Jake Benjamin

Building a Culture of Trust Within the Organization

Deadline: 30 days.

Jake sighed. "I can already tell you the communication problem. Half the time, people don't even know what's going on. Nobody reads emails properly; most just seem to barely skim them and then reply by asking questions about the content of the email they are replying to when the information is in the email!"

"Which is why we need a clear strategy," Kim replied. "I want to roll out leadership communication training. It's not just about what we say—it's how we say it. If we're not aligned, it shows."

Jake chuckled. "You mean we're teaching leaders how to not sound like robots?"

"Exactly," Kim smiled. "We need to make sure that every message we send—whether it's a quick email or a big announcement—aligns with our values and is delivered in a way that feels human."

"We can't do this in a vacuum," Kim said. "Marcella, Max, and Eric need to be part of this, too. Marcella has the final say on transparency initiatives. Max's marketing expertise will help craft internal messaging that feels genuine, and Eric can bring a strategic lens to the Employee Trust Council."

Jake nodded in agreement. "Alright, I'll make sure everyone's looped in. Marcella won't need much convincing—she's always worried about culture. Max might need some coaching on the difference between external marketing and internal comms. But Eric…"

Kim smirked. "Eric's going to love this. It's a strategy challenge."

Craft Your Leadership Trust Strategy

Kim drew three interconnected circles. "Let's map our organizational trust strategy," she began.

Build Trust (Offensive Plays)

"First, we establish internal trust credibility," she explained:

- Employee engagement programs
- Transparency initiatives
- Leadership trust protocols

Protect Trust (Defensive Plays)

Moving to the second circle:

- Internal communication monitoring
- Employee feedback systems
- Cultural health measures

Measure Trust

For the final circle:

Trust Metric	Current	Target
Employee Trust	70%	90%
Leadership Trust	75%	95%
Cultural Health	68%	85%

"Remember," Kim concluded, "internal trust drives external success. Once we roll this out, we should see a direct impact. With transparent leadership, employees will feel more connected to us. The Trust Council will give them a voice, empowering them to take ownership of their work. And clear communication will cut down the confusion."

Jake nodded, now fully engaged. "So, what's the endgame? How will we measure success?"

"Engagement will go up," Kim said confidently. "I'm expecting a 20% increase in employee satisfaction within three months. Turnover will drop, and productivity will rise. But most importantly, we'll have a workforce that trusts us."

Building a Culture of Trust Within the Organization

As Kim left Jake's office, the plan was in place, and she felt a sense of hope. For the first time in a while, it wasn't just about numbers or external reputation—it was about rebuilding the foundation of trust within Rezilify itself. And that, she knew, was the key to real, lasting success.

Steps for the Strategic Leader to Build a Trust Culture:

1. Transparent Leadership:

Objective: Increase leadership visibility.
Tactic: Hold regular forums where employees can engage directly with leadership.
Result: 15% improvement in employee trust metrics within 3 months.

2. Empower Employees:

Objective: Give employees a voice in decision-making.
Tactic: Form an Employee Trust Council.
Result: Boost employee engagement by 20% and reduce turnover.

3. Clear, Consistent Communication:

Objective: Improve internal messaging.
Tactic: Implement leadership communication training.
Result: Achieve alignment between leadership and workforce, increasing satisfaction.

29. The Role of Employee Advocacy in Building Brand Trust

"People trust people more than they trust brands."

- Debbie Millman

As the next strategy session wrapped up, Kim stood at the head of the table, visibly concerned but resolute. "One more thing; there's something crucial we need to discuss—our employee advocacy. It's quietly slipping away, and if we don't act, it could damage more than just internal morale."

Max, usually optimistic, looked surprised. "Our own employees aren't promoting us? Even after our transparency initiatives and all the work we've done on building trust?"

Jake, with his usual sarcasm, muttered, "Maybe they're too focused on their actual work. Just a thought."

Eric, ever the strategist, jumped in. "Jake, this isn't just an afterthought. If our employees don't support us, why should customers? Employee advocacy is an essential trust signal."

Kim nodded. "Exactly. Our employees are our most credible advocates. But they won't naturally share our story if they feel disconnected or unsupported."

"We've been investing so much in trust-building with our clients," Kim added. "But we've missed an opportunity here. If our employees aren't engaged, the gap in trust extends to every customer interaction they have."

Max looked thoughtful. "So how do we solve this? What's our first move?"

Kim pulled up a slide on her laptop, showing recent examples of effective employee advocacy. "Microsoft, in early 2024, revamped their employee advocacy strategy with an internal content-sharing platform. They saw a 40% increase in employee engagement and a boost in brand visibility across B2B channels by 50%. The key was making content accessible and aligned with both company goals and employee values."

Eric nodded. "And Salesforce's 2024 initiative involved a content hub for employees that didn't just encourage them to share company news—it connected to their own roles and interests. Employee-shared content received eight times more engagement than company-shared posts. Making it easy and relevant is everything."

Jake, ever the realist, asked, "So, it's about providing authentic content employees can get behind. But who's handling this?"

Max responded quickly, "I'll head up the development of an internal content hub. We'll create customizable options that align with employees' personal and professional interests. This way, they'll be genuinely excited to share."

Kim looked at Eric. "We also need a meaningful incentive program—something that doesn't feel superficial. It has to be personal, like PTO, team-building experiences, and real-time recognition."

Eric leaned in, smiling. "Count me in. Adobe's latest initiative was huge. Their approach made rewards part of their culture, not just a one-time program. Participation soared, and their employee satisfaction increased by 30%."

"Good," Kim said. "And Jake, we need you to lead training on authenticity. We want employees to share real, personal stories—content that actually reflects their experiences here at Rezilify. Google did this with their 2024 workshops, and it led to a 45% increase in trust metrics. It's about making the message human."

Jake frowned, skeptical. "So we're asking employees to be advocates but in their own words. I guess similar to what we did to empower them with the social media thing. That's better than scripted posts, but let's be careful it doesn't come off as fake."

"Exactly," Kim replied. "It needs to be real. The goal here is authenticity, not propaganda. If they believe in it, customers will, too."

Kim glanced around the table. "Here's the plan for the next 60 days:"

Plan for Encouraging Employee Brand Advocacy

1. **Internal Content Hub**

    - *Objective*: Make it easy for employees to access and share personalized, brand-aligned content.
    - *Owner:* Max
    - *Deadline:* 30 days to launch.

2. **Meaningful Rewards Program**

    - *Objective:* Develop a rewards program that genuinely motivates employees to engage with the brand.
    - *Owner:* Eric
    - *Deadline*: 45 days to roll out.

3. **Authenticity Training**

    - *Objective:* Equip employees with storytelling skills for sharing genuine, relatable experiences.
    - *Owner:* Jake
    - *Deadline:* 60 days to implement.

Craft Your Leadership Trust Strategy

Kim drew three interconnected circles. "Here's our employee advocacy trust blueprint," she began.

Build Trust (Offensive Plays)

"First, we establish employee advocacy credibility," she explained:

- Employee ambassador programs
- Internal storytelling initiatives
- Social media advocacy systems

Protect Trust (Defensive Plays)

Moving to the second circle:

- Advocacy monitoring protocols
- Message consistency checks
- Employee protection measures

Building a Culture of Trust Within the Organization

Measure Trust

For the final circle:

Trust Metric	Current	Target
Employee Advocacy	70%	90%
Message Impact	75%	95%
Brand Alignment	68%	85%

"Remember," Kim concluded, "authentic employee voices build lasting trust."

* * * *

Forty-five days later, the team reconvened, eager to review the results. Kim led the meeting with a renewed sense of optimism.

Max started. "The content hub is live, and we're seeing real traction. Over 60% of employees have used it, and brand mentions are up by 20%, all through employee-driven content. It's already impacting our visibility metrics in B2B channels."

Eric added, "Our rewards program has taken off. Employees are actively competing for recognition, and we've seen a 25% increase in internal engagement with company initiatives. It's transforming our culture."

Jake, who had been cautious at first, shared his progress. "The authenticity training went over better than I expected. Employees are bringing real stories to the table, and our external trust metrics reflect a 12% improvement. I underestimated how much they'd appreciate this approach."

Kim looked around the table, clearly pleased. "We're on the right track. These changes show how investing in our own people turns them into our biggest advocates. It's genuine, and customers can feel the difference."

Jake, surprised at the effectiveness, nodded. "When employees believe, it's contagious. Our engagement metrics reflect it, and even customer feedback highlights a noticeable improvement."

Eric, always strategic, added, "And that authenticity? It sets us apart. Clients are seeing us not just as another vendor but as a trusted partner with genuine advocates."

Kim smiled. "Great work, team. We're building something that extends beyond traditional marketing. Let's keep this momentum going, focusing on both internal trust and external transparency. This is just the beginning."

Building a Culture of Trust Within the Organization

Comparative Trust Metrics and Industry Data (2024)

- **Internal Engagement:** Increase employee engagement from 45% to 60% with the content hub.
- **Brand Visibility:** 50% boost in brand visibility within B2B networks.
- **Trust and Satisfaction Metrics**: A 12% improvement in external trust metrics as reported in customer feedback.
- **Employee Advocacy Engagement**: Raised from baseline levels to a 25% increase in active participation due to the incentive program.
- **Customer Trust Response:** Direct positive feedback from customers indicates a higher sense of partnership trust, with employee-driven content showing 8x engagement over traditional corporate posts.

By implementing these strategies, Kim felt relieved that this ensured not only that employees felt engaged but also that they became authentic advocates, helping to close the trust gap and strengthen both internal morale and external credibility in a competitive B2B environment.

Steps for the Strategic Leader to Encourage Employee Advocacy:

1. **Create an Employee Advocacy Platform:** Build a user-friendly internal hub where employees can access and share content that aligns with both company values and their personal beliefs.
2. **Incentivize Participation:** Offer meaningful rewards such as additional time off, gift cards, or public recognition to motivate employees to engage in advocacy efforts.
3. **Train for Authenticity:** Host training sessions to help employees craft personal, genuine stories about their experiences with the company—authenticity builds trust.
4. **Foster Transparency:** Ensure employees have access to clear, open communication about company decisions and initiatives. Authentic leadership creates engaged, loyal advocates.

30. Trust and Employee Relationships: Internal Trust Building for External Success

"You have to create a culture where everybody has an opportunity to be recognized."

-John Mackey

The mood in the executive lounge was tense as Kim cleared her throat for another impromptu discussion. Recent numbers from both employee engagement and customer satisfaction had raised red flags—signs that internal trust wasn't where it needed to be.

Max kicked things off, his usual laid-back demeanor now tinged with frustration. "Internal trust? Really? We've been firing off engagement surveys like confetti every quarter. What happened to the rewards incentive program? Didn't that change things? I thought we had that covered."

Eric was also less patient today. He had other things he was supposed to be doing right now. "Surveys and incentives don't equal trust, Max. Employees can be engaged in their work and still feel like management doesn't have their back. There's a huge difference. Trust is deeper."

Kim nodded, arms crossed, as she added, "Exactly. Just look at Zappos. They built trust internally, and it flows into how their employees treat customers. We're not seeing that same trust here—and it's showing in our external reputation."

Max snorted. "So, what? Do we need to hug our employees now?"

Kim stopped him, her tone sharp but measured. "It's not about hugs, Max. It's about creating a culture where employees feel heard and valued. Right now, there's a gap between what we say and what we do. Trust erodes when that gap widens."

Jake leaned forward, his analytical mind now engaged. "It's true. Zappos saw a 30% jump in customer satisfaction after empowering their employees to make decisions. We've got the data to show our customers can tell something's off with us—and it's going to keep affecting our bottom line if we don't fix it."

Eric's sarcasm slipped in. "So, Max, ready to hand over the marketing reins to the interns yet?"

Max shot back, "Oh yeah, sure. What could go wrong?"

Kim sighed. "Let's focus. Trust is earned through action. Right now, employees don't trust us because they don't feel empowered. Sure, we're throwing all sorts of information and incentives at them, but they think we're not listening."

"Absolutely. We need solutions and fast." Jake interrupted, worried about the hit to the bottom line. "Eric, can you set up an anonymous feedback system? Something where employees can voice concerns without fear of backlash. We want to know what's really going on beneath the surface."

Eric nodded. "On it. Good plan; I'll model it after Google's feedback system. We'll make sure everyone knows their voices matter."

Kim turned to Max. "You're up next. What do you think about giving frontline employees more decision-making power? Let them feel ownership over their roles. Can you design a plan that gives them real autonomy?"

Max rolled his eyes, but he was already thinking. "Okay, I'll make it work. But no one's messing with my budget."

Jake smirked. "I wouldn't dream of it. Kim, why don't you take the initiative to address the underlying trust issues? Set up focus groups, create spaces where employees can have candid conversations, and get to the heart of their concerns."

Kim nodded. "Consider it done. We'll use this to identify areas where trust is weak and target those with actionable solutions."

Jake continued, "If we do this right, the numbers will follow. But it has to be real. No surface-level fixes."

Kim's tone was firm. "Exactly. This is about rebuilding trust from the ground up. Let's meet again in 45 days to assess our progress."

Craft Your Leadership Trust Strategy

Max drew three interconnected circles. "Let's map our internal trust strategy," he began.

Build Trust (Offensive Plays)

"First, we establish internal credibility," he explained:

- Employee engagement programs
- Internal communication systems
- Leadership transparency initiatives

Protect Trust (Defensive Plays)

Moving to the second circle:

- Internal feedback monitoring
- Employee satisfaction tracking
- Cultural health measures

Measure Trust

For the final circle:

Trust Metric	Current	Target
Employee Trust	70%	90%
Internal Communication	75%	95%
Leadership Credibility	68%	85%

"Remember," Max concluded, "internal trust drives external success."

* * * *

When they reconvened later to dissect their actions, the atmosphere in the room was notably lighter. The team had worked hard, and now it was time to review the results. Kim had conferred with Marcella and she joined them to hear the results.

Marcella gestured to Eric. "Alright, Eric, how did the feedback system work out?"

Eric grinned. "Better than I expected. We've already seen a 15% increase in employee satisfaction. People feel like their concerns are being taken seriously, and we've caught issues that were flying under the radar."

Jake nodded, still a little skeptical. "Okay, but what about the autonomy thing? Did we unleash chaos?"

Max straightened, looking surprisingly satisfied. "Not at all. We gave the frontline marketing team more decision-making power, and customer interactions have improved by 20%. They're coming up with ideas I wouldn't have thought of. It turns out, when people feel trusted, they deliver."

Jake leaned forward, nodding in approval. "That's not just marketing. Customer satisfaction across the board is up. It's clear that happier employees lead to happier customers."

Marcella turned to Kim. "Kim, how did your focus groups go?"

Kim smiled. "They were a game-changer. Employees were brutally honest about where we were falling short. But here's the thing—once they saw we were listening and making changes, the trust started to rebuild. Leadership trust metrics are up 10%, and employees are more willing to speak out now."

Marcella leaned back, clearly pleased. "This is the kind of progress we needed. But we're not done. Building internal trust is a journey, not a one-time project."

Max, ever the joker, smirked. "So, are we hugging the employees yet?"

Kim shot back, laughing, "Only if you want a lawsuit, Max."

The team chuckled, but the mood was one of determination. They had made progress, but there was more to do. As they left the room, there was a renewed sense of purpose—a commitment to making trust a permanent part of Rezilify's culture.

Steps For the Strategic Leader to Build Internal Trust:

1. **Implement Anonymous Feedback Systems**: Create channels where employees can voice concerns without fear of repercussions. Act on the feedback to show you're listening.
2. **Empower Employees:** Give teams more autonomy, especially on the front lines. Let them make decisions and own their roles. This leads to higher engagement and better customer interactions.
3. **Host Focus Groups:** Facilitate open conversations where employees can share their thoughts and experiences. Use these insights to target specific areas where trust needs to be rebuilt.
4. **Lead by Example:** Leadership should model transparency, accountability, and follow-through. Trust is earned when actions match words.

By taking these steps, you'll not only improve internal trust but also strengthen your external reputation—because trust starts from within.

31. Employee and Employer Trust Statistics

"Trust and mutual value creation help both employer and employee compete in the marketplace."

—Reid Hoffman, Founder of LinkedIn

The executive lounge at Rezilify was quiet in the early morning light. Marcella, coffee in hand, sat near the window, scrolling through her phone as she looked out over the city. Kim entered and sat across from her, sensing something on Marcella's mind.

"Penny for your thoughts?" Kim asked, breaking the silence.

Marcella looked up, setting her phone aside. "Just thinking about trust. Jake pulled some numbers the other day that were pretty eye-opening—it's not just our customers; it's our employees, too. Trust seems to affect everything."

Kim nodded, taking a sip of her coffee. "Absolutely. I think after all the efforts we've made recently, it's really brought home how easy it is to overlook how much internal trust impacts the bigger picture. People tend to think of branding in terms of customers, but what about employer branding? That's just as critical."

Marcella leaned forward. "Jake mentioned that 80% of talent acquisition managers believe employer branding plays a huge role in building trust and recruitment. People want more than just a paycheck; they want to work for a company they believe in. Have you seen that shift in our recent hires?"

"Definitely," Kim agreed. "The conversations I've had in interviews have changed. Candidates now ask about our culture and values. They're not just looking for perks—they want to know how we treat our people and if they can trust us to support their growth."

"In that same conversation, he also mentioned that companies with strong employer brands see a 28% reduction in turnover," Marcella added thoughtfully. "That's huge, Kim. If we can retain our people longer, we don't just save on recruitment costs; we keep the institutional knowledge that makes us stronger."

Kim nodded, setting her coffee down. "I would be inclined to agree. That's where the real value lies. When employees trust us, they're less likely to leave. Engaged employees become our best advocates—their loyalty shows in every client interaction and the way they talk about us to potential hires. It's like we're planting seeds of trust that grow into lasting loyalty."

"That's right," Marcella said, reaching for her tablet. "The statistics across multiple industries back it up, too. Check it out." She handed Kim her tablet.

Employee and Employer Trust Statistics

Key Workplace Trust Statistics (2024)

Overall Trust Metrics

- Employee trust in leadership: 48% (down from 55% in 2023)
- Importance of trust in job satisfaction: 72%
- Willingness to leave an untrusted employer: 85%
- Increase in remote work trust since 2023: 28%

Industry-Specific Trust Data

- Technology Sector:
    - Leadership Trust: 62%
    - Data transparency: 58%
    - Job security confidence: 65%
    - Remote work trust: 82%

- Financial Services:
    - Leadership Trust: 54%
    - Data transparency: 71%
    - Job security confidence: 59%
    - Remote work trust: 67%

- Healthcare:
    - Leadership Trust: 68%
    - Data transparency: 75%
    - Job security confidence: 72%
    - Remote work trust: 64%

Comparative Analysis

- Trust by Company Size:

    o Small companies (up to 100): 72% trust rating
    o Mid-size (100-1000): 65% trust rating
    o Enterprise (1000+): 52% trust rating

- Trust by Leadership Level:

    o Direct supervisors: 76% trust
    o Middle management: 58% trust
    o Executive leadership: 45% trust
    o Board level: 38% trust

Impact on Business Metrics

High-Trust Organizations:

- 74% less stress
- 106% more energy at work
- 50% higher productivity
- 13% fewer sick days
- 76% higher engagement

Low-Trust Organizations:

- 45% higher turnover
- 32% lower productivity
- 28% higher stress levels
- 18% lower revenue per employee

Employee and Employer Trust Statistics

Key Trust Drivers

- Most Important Factors:
    - Transparency in communication (82%)
    - Fair compensation (78%)
    - Work-life balance (76%)
    - Career development (72%)
    - Job security (68%)

Success Metrics for High-Trust Organizations

- Employee satisfaction: Target > 85%
- Trust in leadership: Target > 75%
- Retention rate: Target > 90%
- Engagement score: Target > 80%

Marcella got up to refill her coffee, the gears in her mind turning. "It's not just about retention. When people feel valued and trusted, they become so invested that they naturally help build our reputation. Externally, that translates to a stronger brand that attracts more top talent."

"Exactly," Kim said. "Internally, we build trust, which boosts engagement and lowers turnover. Externally, that reputation attracts the best people, creating a cycle of growth and loyalty. But it only works if we nurture it."

Marcella smirked. "Jake actually called it a 'trust flywheel.' It's easy to forget that internal trust and external perception are connected."

"They're inseparable," Kim agreed. "We can't expect clients to trust us if our employees don't. Their confidence—or lack of it—shines through in every customer interaction. When our people believe in us and feel trusted, that radiates outward."

Marcella settled back in her chair. "So, the next step is ensuring we live up to our talk on trust. I want our employer brand to resonate with our current team, including our remote teams, and the talent we want to attract."

"To do that, we need transparency. We can look at aspects of the GUARDIAN Framework for that," Kim replied. "Employees want to know where we're headed and why. They also need a voice in that process. Giving them a seat at the table is the cornerstone of building trust."

"And when they feel like they belong, they stop looking for the exit," Marcella added.

Marcella reached over to her tablet and pulled out a stylus; she drew three interconnected circles. "Here's our employee trust blueprint," she began.

Craft Your Leadership Trust Strategy

Build Trust (Offensive Plays)

"First, we establish workplace trust credibility," she explained:

- Employee feedback systems
- Leadership transparency programs

- Performance recognition initiatives

Protect Trust (Defensive Plays)

Moving to the second circle:

- Employee satisfaction monitoring
- Workplace culture protection
- Trust verification systems

Measure Trust

For the final circle:

Trust Metric	Current	Target
Employee Trust	70%	90%
Leadership Trust	75%	95%
Workplace Culture	68%	85%

"Remember," Marcella concluded, "employee trust drives organizational success."

"Exactly," Kim said. "If we invest in our people, they'll invest in us."

Marcella raised her coffee cup toward Kim. "Here's to building and keeping the trust flywheel spinning."

Kim clinked her cup with Marcella's. "And to create a legacy of trust that benefits everyone."

Steps for the Strategic Leader to Build Employer Trust:

1. **Strengthen Employer Branding:** Communicate your company's values and culture to prospective hires. A strong employer brand attracts top talent and demonstrates trustworthiness to employees and recruits.

2. **Reduce Turnover with Trust:** Transparent communication and employee empowerment lead to a 28% decrease in turnover, saving on recruitment and training costs.

3. **Foster Employee Advocacy:** Encourage employee engagement by valuing their input and fostering a supportive environment. Employees who believe in the organization become its most powerful advocates, enhancing external reputation.

4. **Transparency and Communication:** Maintain open communication and involve employees in decision-making processes. This bolsters internal trust and externally presents an authentic, trustworthy image.

32. Building Trust in Hybrid Work Environments

"The only thing worse than being blind is having sight but no vision."

—Helen Keller

Later that day, Kim caught up with Eric as he strode briskly down the hallway at Rezilify, heading toward the elevator. "Can I pick your brain for a minute?" she asked.

"Sure, I'm heading down to Finance. You're welcome to walk with me. What's on your mind?" Eric replied, keeping his stride steady.

"I was talking to Marcella this morning about the trust issues with our employees," Kim said, glancing at him. "I was thinking about the concerns from the remote managers too, and it's becoming clear that communication alone isn't cutting it."

Eric nodded thoughtfully as they waited for the elevator. "It's true. Communication is just the start. But what people need most is transparency, especially when they're remote."

"Exactly. It's not just about keeping people in the loop; it's about giving them a reason to trust what they hear. Buffer figured this out years ago—they have an open policies approach with clearly defined expectations. Maybe we could incorporate some of those principles."

As they stepped into the elevator, Kim's expression turned pensive. "But how do we tailor it to us? We're not all-remote like Buffer. We've got hybrid teams too, and I think something like Salesforce's bi-weekly check-ins could help, but we need to customize it."

Eric gave a quick nod of agreement. "You're right. No cookie-cutter solutions here. We have to be deliberate—intentional—especially about setting expectations."

As Kim and Eric discussed a strategy, they realized how crucial it was to address not just team morale but the nuanced psychology behind trust-building in remote settings.

"We can't overlook how the nature of remote work itself can lead to isolation," Eric noted. "Our policy needs to account for more than just logistical transparency. We need to make the team feel involved and invested in a way that's unique to our remote structure."

"Right," Kim agreed. "The key is keeping a steady rhythm of interaction. It's easy for remote team members to feel like they're on an island, especially when everyone is focused on their own tasks. That's why those bi-weekly check-ins are so essential; they're more than a formality—they're a time to reconnect, address issues head-on, and make sure everyone feels seen."

Eric added, "Another thing we should consider is setting up a feedback loop specifically for remote teams. If we're expecting trust to thrive, they need to know their voices are being heard as well—whether it's about processes, workload, or the team-building activities."

Kim nodded thoughtfully, "Of course. Much like for our in-house employees, an anonymous feedback system could work here, giving people a comfortable channel to express their thoughts without feeling judged. And that feedback needs to go both ways. If leadership is sharing goals and being transparent about challenges, the team will feel more aligned."

They reviewed additional steps to create a virtual work culture aligned with their in-house trust goals. One new idea came up: a digital recognition system. "Why not implement something that rewards collaboration and proactive communication?" Eric suggested. "Even a simple monthly recognition for remote team contributions can help people feel more engaged."

"That's a smart idea," Kim responded, jotting it down. "We can track engagement levels around the recognition program and make it a part of our KPIs for this project."

As they prepared to share these new elements with the rest of the team, Eric summed up their approach: "This isn't just about managing people remotely; it's about creating a remote culture that breeds trust. Every metric we track—from engagement to feedback rates—will tell us if we're truly achieving that."

Kim's eyes lit up as ideas sparked. "I'll draft a remote work policy that spells it all out: what's expected of the team and what they can expect from leadership. No guessing games."

"Smart move. Guesswork is a trust killer. And we can't afford to let morale slip—as we've seen, internal trust leaks into customer trust."

They exited the elevator and headed to Jake's office. Jake greeted them from his desk. "Hey, you two, what's going on?"

"We're strategizing ways to build trust with our remote teams," Kim replied. "Marcella's behind it, but we need concrete steps. Got a few minutes to go over it?"

Jake leaned back in his chair. "Absolutely. Let's hash it out."

Kim settled into a chair. "Here's where things stand: We'll get Max piloting bi-weekly check-ins, Eric working on a transparency-focused policy, and how about you leading the team-building piece?"

Jake gave a grin. "I'm ahead of you there. I found some great ideas from GitLab—things like virtual and hybrid team-building events that aren't just 'fluff.' I'm thinking we start with a trivia night, then expand if that resonates."

"Perfect," Eric chimed in, leaning on Jake's desk. "But don't make it cheesy. Forced engagement kills authenticity."

Jake chuckled, "Got it—no forced fun. I'll focus on something genuine. We'll test it out within 60 days to gauge interest and engagement."

"And the remote policy should be finalized within the same timeframe," Eric said. "Forty-five days to draft, with input from the teams. We need it ironclad, so expectations are rock-solid."

Kim glanced at the calendar on Jake's wall. "Good. I'll keep an eye on morale. If trust doesn't improve internally, it'll affect how we serve our customers—and they'll feel it."

Jake nodded. "We need metrics too. I'll monitor engagement levels from the team-building side, but we'll need data across the board—how's engagement in the check-ins? How's productivity after the policy launch? Every piece matters."

Craft Your Leadership Trust Strategy

Eric drew three interconnected circles. "Let's map our hybrid work trust strategy," he began.

Build Trust (Offensive Plays)

"First, we establish hybrid workplace credibility," he explained:

- Remote work trust protocols
- Digital collaboration systems
- Virtual team-building initiatives

Protect Trust (Defensive Plays)

Moving to the second circle:

- Remote productivity monitoring
- Digital security measures
- Team engagement tracking

Measure Trust

For the final circle:

Trust Metric	Current	Target
Remote Trust	70%	90%
Team Cohesion	75%	95%
Digital Security	68%	85%

"Remember," he concluded, "hybrid trust requires both digital and human connection."

Eric crossed his arms, deep in thought. "Let's look at the bigger picture, too. When internal trust is strong, it ripples outward. Our customers feel it, and potential hires see it. That's the real value of all this."

Kim smiled, feeling the momentum of the conversation. "Exactly. If our remote people believe in us, that trust projects outward. It impacts everything—from employee retention to our reputation as an employer and a trusted partner."

Jake glanced at his watch and stood up. "Alright, sounds like we've got our plan: bi-weekly check-ins to keep the communication steady, a clear remote work policy to eliminate guesswork, and authentic team-building events to reinforce our culture. We've got 60 days to see measurable results."

"Let's make sure it sticks," Kim added, standing. "Otherwise, we'll be back here in a few months dealing with the same issues."

Eric gave a small smirk, raising an eyebrow. "No pressure then."

Kim laughed. "Just a little bit."

Steps for the Strategic Leader to Build Trust in Remote Work Environments

1. Develop Transparent Communication Protocols

- Set up daily or weekly check-ins to keep everyone informed.
- Use collaboration tools to make project progress visible and accessible.
- Establish clear remote work policies, outlining expectations for response times, deliverables, and availability.

2. Establish Goals and Expectations

- Set clear objectives and KPIs that define success in the virtual workspace.
- Align team goals with individual roles so that everyone understands their contribution.

- Regularly update goals to reflect changes and ensure everyone is focused on the same outcomes.

3. Build Accountability Systems

- Use project management software for transparent tracking and updates.
- Assign responsibility for key tasks and hold periodic reviews to discuss progress.
- Establish channels for constructive feedback, both peer-to-peer and from leadership.

4. Foster Virtual Team Culture

- Organize regular team-building events that foster connection and engagement.
- Encourage peer recognition through public shout-outs or virtual badges.
- Allow space for informal socialization to maintain a human element in the digital workspace.

5. Implement Trust-Building Initiatives

- Facilitate regular one-on-ones between managers and team members.
- Open feedback channels to gather input on remote work experience and challenges.
- Use clear performance metrics, reinforcing a merit-based, transparent work environment.

6. Continuously Measure Trust Levels

- Track engagement, response times, project completion rates, and collaboration.

- Survey employees on the quality of communication, psychological safety, and social cohesion.
- Analyze trust metrics, like engagement scores and retention rates, to measure improvement.

7. Prepare a Trust Recovery Framework for Missteps

- Address any breaches of trust immediately with transparency and empathy.
- Take corrective action, such as revisiting unclear policies or improving tools.
- Use feedback from these situations to strengthen future trust-building efforts.

8. Balance Autonomy with Accountability

- Allow flexibility in work hours or methods, emphasizing outcomes over rigid processes.
- Ensure team members feel empowered to own their work while staying aligned with organizational goals.
- Maintain consistent, open communication, bridging gaps between autonomy and accountability.

33. Maintaining Trust During Major Organizational Changes

"Change is inevitable. Growth is optional."

— John C. Maxwell

The news of a major reorganization within Rezilify had left the executive team buzzing with anticipation—and a healthy dose of trepidation. As Kim walked into Jake's office, she could sense the gravity of the situation reflected in his gaze as he stared at a spreadsheet, lines of data populating the screen.

"Got a minute?" she asked, settling into a chair opposite him.

Jake looked up, raising an eyebrow. "For you? Always. Let me guess: the reorg?"

"Bingo." Kim sighed. "It's got everyone's nerves frayed. I've been thinking a lot about how we can keep trust levels steady through the transition."

"Good call," Jake replied, folding his arms. "Reorgs always stir up uncertainty. Employees get wary of changes to teams, roles, and expectations. If we're not careful, this could spiral into a morale issue—and once that happens, trust becomes a casualty."

"Exactly. I've been researching some companies that pulled this off with minimal trust erosion. Take Microsoft, for instance. Back in 2014, they went through a massive restructuring under Satya Nadella's new leadership. One of his first moves was to establish a 'growth mindset' across the company and prioritize empathy in management," Kim explained. "By actively communicating that people's contributions would still matter, Nadella set a tone of respect and recognition. They saw increased engagement, and trust didn't tank as it typically does during a reorg."

Jake nodded thoughtfully. "I remember that. Nadella wasn't shy about laying out his vision, either. When leaders don't share their goals, people can feel lost. At least if we're clear, employees will know what we're aiming for and their role in it. Look at Netflix and their shift to streaming—the same thing. Reed Hastings was transparent about the shift, setting clear expectations and letting people see the big picture. They avoided a trust breakdown by letting employees feel invested in the change, not just pushed along with it."

Kim leaned forward, excited. "That's the key: making employees feel like they're participants in the change, not bystanders. It reminds me of something Cisco did a few years ago when they reorganized to focus on cybersecurity. They brought in employees for feedback during the process, especially in areas impacted by the shift. It wasn't just top-down changes—it was collaborative, and that made people feel respected."

Maintaining Trust During Major Organizational Changes

Jake nodded, jotting down notes. "We'll need to do something similar. Make sure people see themselves in this change. I'm thinking we should launch an 'Impact Feedback' initiative. We can set up dedicated channels for anonymous employee input so people feel safe and honest. And maybe bi-weekly Q&A sessions with Marcella to address concerns openly."

"Good thinking. And what about empowering middle management?" Kim added. "They're the ones who directly interact with the teams daily. When Twitter was restructured in 2021, it focused on training middle managers to be 'change ambassadors.' Those managers became trusted points of contact, and their teams had someone to turn to. It humanized the process."

"Yeah, I can see how that would work here," Jake replied. "If our managers are trained to lead with empathy and transparency, that trust will trickle down."

Kim leaned back, deep in thought. "We should also recognize people's efforts through the change. Positive reinforcement goes a long way. During Amazon's restructuring in 2020, they implemented a system of incremental rewards—small bonuses for those who hit transition milestones, performance recognition, that kind of thing."

"Good point," Jake agreed. "People don't just need a vision—they need to feel like their hard work is acknowledged. It's easy to ask for resilience, but without a little reward, people get fatigued."

The two sat in silence for a moment, letting the pieces fall into place. Finally, Jake summarized, "So here's the game plan: set up anonymous feedback channels, bring managers into the fold as change ambassadors, schedule regular Q&A sessions with Marcella, and create a recognition system to celebrate achievements throughout the transition."

Craft Your Leadership Trust Strategy:

Jake drew three interconnected circles. "Here's our organizational change trust blueprint," he began.

Build Trust (Offensive Plays)

"First, we establish change management credibility," he explained:

- Change communication programs
- Leadership transparency initiatives
- Employee engagement systems

Protect Trust (Defensive Plays)

Moving to the second circle:

- Change impact monitoring
- Employee feedback loops
- Culture protection measures

Maintaining Trust During Major Organizational Changes

Measure Trust

For the final circle:

Trust Metric	Current	Target
Change Trust	70%	90%
Employee Confidence	75%	95%
Cultural Stability	68%	85%

"Remember," Jake concluded, "trust is the bridge between change and success."

Kim grinned, "Exactly. I'll draft a proposal with the details and present it to Marcella. If we pull this off right, we won't just maintain trust—we might even strengthen it."

Steps for the Strategic Leader to Strengthen Trust During Organizational Change:

1. Communicate Vision and Purpose:

Set clear goals for the reorganization so employees understand the "why" behind the changes. Align everyone on a shared mission, emphasizing how each role contributes to the future state. Establishing clear goals for reorganization is essential to help employees understand the "why" behind the changes. Aligning everyone on a shared mission emphasizes how each role contributes to the organization's future state.

For example, in March 2024, Citigroup CEO Jane Fraser announced a comprehensive restructuring aimed at simplifying operations and enhancing efficiency. The reorganization focused on core strengths in Services, Markets, Banking, Wealth, and U.S. Personal Banking. Fraser communicated a clear vision, emphasizing the need for belief in the bank's new path and acknowledging past shortcomings. She urged employees to embrace the changes and support each other, highlighting how each role would contribute to the firm's strategic objectives.

2. Incorporate Employee Feedback Loops:

Establishing dedicated channels for anonymous employee feedback allows for honest, constructive input during organizational changes. This approach ensures that employees feel heard and valued, fostering a sense of inclusion and ownership in the transformation process.

For example, Cisco's 2024 Reorganization: In August 2024, Cisco Systems announced a significant restructuring, including a 7% reduction in its workforce, to focus on high-growth areas such as artificial intelligence and cybersecurity. The company faced internal challenges, with reports of a toxic work environment and low employee morale.

3. Empower Middle Managers as Change Ambassadors:

Training middle management to act as consistent, trusted points of contact for employees fosters open communication and support during organizational changes. This approach ensures that employees receive clear information and feel supported throughout transitions. In September 2024, Amazon announced plans to reduce the number of supervisors to increase the ratio of individual contributors to managers, aiming to operate more like a startup and streamline processes. This restructuring effort involved flattening departments and asking senior leadership teams to increase the ratio of individual contributors to managers by at least 15% by the end of the first quarter of 2025.

To facilitate this transition, Amazon empowered middle managers to act as change ambassadors. They were trained to provide teams with a steady, empathetic presence, ensuring that employees felt supported and informed throughout the restructuring process. This strategy helped maintain morale and productivity during significant organizational changes.

4. Institute Regular Leadership Q&A Sessions:

To foster a culture of openness and accountability, companies can benefit from holding regular Q&A sessions with senior leadership. These sessions provide employees a direct line to leadership, addressing concerns transparently and reinforcing trust.

For example: Reed Hastings' Transparency During Netflix's Shift to Streaming. As Netflix embarked on its ambitious shift to streaming, CEO Reed Hastings recognized the importance of clear, consistent communication. He instituted bi-weekly Q&A sessions, where employees could voice questions and hear directly from senior leaders about the company's strategy, challenges, and vision. Hastings' openness in addressing employee concerns was instrumental during this period of transformation, as Netflix navigated uncharted waters and adapted to a new digital landscape.

"Reed didn't shy away from hard questions," Kim explained, gesturing to the slide. "He tackled concerns head-on, discussing both the risks and the opportunities of streaming. This level of transparency showed employees they weren't in the dark—he trusted them enough to share the good and the bad."

Jake nodded in agreement. "That's what made the difference. Those regular Q&As weren't just updates; they were a dialogue. Employees felt like they were part of the journey and understood how their roles contributed to the company's future."

5. Celebrate Incremental Wins:

Implementing a recognition program to honor contributions and milestones reached during a transition can boost morale and reinforce a sense of progress. Celebrating these incremental wins helps employees feel valued and keeps motivation high as the organization moves through changes.

For example: Amazon's incremental reward system during its 2024 transformation. In 2024, as Amazon navigated a major organizational transformation, the company recognized the need to keep employee morale strong amid the shift. They introduced an incremental reward system, spotlighting resilience and accomplishments at each stage of the transition. Rather than waiting for the end of the process to acknowledge efforts, Amazon celebrated every step forward—whether it was a new initiative launch, process improvement, or team goal achieved.

"Amazon understood that large-scale change can feel overwhelming," Kim noted. "By highlighting these smaller victories, they showed employees that every contribution mattered and that they were part of something meaningful."

Jake added, "It wasn't just about hitting big milestones. Amazon's program recognized the day-to-day wins, reinforcing a culture of progress and resilience."

PART VII: MEASURING AND QUANTIFYING TRUST

34. Visual and Design Trust Statistics

"Design is the silent ambassador of your brand."

— Paul Rand

Max and Eric walked through the marketing department, pausing occasionally to greet colleagues and exchange ideas. Their conversation flowed as they made their way to the elevator.

"You know, Eric, I've been waiting for us to dive into this visual trust thing. People underestimate how much design impacts the way customers see us."

"Yeah, but you're the design guy. What's the big deal? We've had the same logo for years, and people seem to like it." Eric glanced up from his phone.

"It's more than the logo. It's the whole package—colors, fonts, layouts. We're talking about a subconscious judgment here. Did you know it only takes 50 milliseconds for someone to form an opinion about our brand based on what they see?"

Eric looked at him and cocked one eyebrow "Fifty milliseconds? So, if they hate what they see, we've lost them before we've even had a chance to tell them anything?"

"Exactly. People are visual creatures. If our design is inconsistent or confusing, they'll assume we're unreliable in everything else, too. It's all about trust—and design is a big part of that."

Eric chuckled. "Trust through colors and fonts. Who would've thought? So, what, if we slap a few nice colors together, we're golden?"

"I wish it were that easy. It's not just about what looks good—it's about what those colors *mean*. For instance, 90% of product assessments are influenced by color alone. Blue, for example, signals trust and stability, which is why you see it everywhere in banking and tech."

Eric scoffed, "So if we decided to go with red instead, we'd be telling people we're running a clearance sale?"

Max grinned. "Pretty much. Colors create emotional responses, and emotions drive decisions. Blue says, 'We've got your back.' Red says, 'Hurry, buy now!' If we want people to trust us with their data, we need to stick with blue and gray—colors that evoke security and professionalism."

Eric leaned against the elevator wall. "Makes sense. But what about consistency? Is it really that big of a deal if our website looks a bit different from our social media?"

"Absolutely. Consistency is everything. It's how people recognize us. Studies show that 80% of brand recognition is tied to visual design. If someone sees one version of our brand on LinkedIn and another on our website, it sends the wrong message. It makes us look sloppy—like we don't have our act together."

Eric nodded. "Makes sense, if we can't keep our own brand consistent, why should customers trust us to keep their data secure? Got it."

"Exactly. It's a simple thing, but it has a huge impact." They exited the elevator. "Look at brands like Apple or Capital One. They're consistent across every platform, and it builds trust without them having to say a word."

Eric glanced at Max. "That also makes sense. So, what's next? A full brand makeover?"

"No need for a complete overhaul. We're already using the right colors and design elements, but we need to tighten up. I'll be in charge of making sure every visual touchpoint—our website, emails, and ads—tells the same story. That's how we build trust, especially in a field like cybersecurity."

Craft Your Executive Strategy:

Max drew three interconnected circles. "Let's map our visual trust strategy," he began.

Build Trust (Offensive Plays)

"First, we establish visual credibility," he explained:

- Design trust elements
- Visual consistency programs
- Brand authenticity systems

Protect Trust (Defensive Plays)

Moving to the second circle:

- Design integrity monitoring
- Visual consistency checks
- Brand protection measures

Measure Trust

For the final circle:

Trust Metric	Current	Target
Visual Trust	70%	90%
Design Consistency	75%	95%
Brand Recognition	68%	85%

"Remember," Max concluded, "visual trust is the first impression of credibility."

"Alright, I'm sold. Just make sure I don't have to look at 500 shades of blue, okay?" Eric teased.

Max laughed. "Don't worry. I'll keep it simple but effective. Every element matters, but we'll keep it cohesive."

Steps for the Strategic Leader to Build Trust through Visual Design:

1. **Ensure Consistency Across All Platforms:** From social media to websites and ads, every visual element should be consistent. This builds brand recognition and reinforces trust.

2. **Leverage Color Psychology:** Use colors that align with your brand values. For industries like tech and finance, blue signals trust and stability, while red might be more appropriate for urgency-driven promotions.

3. **Simplify and Streamline Visual Identity:** Every design element—logo, typography, layout—should work together to tell the same story. A cohesive design reduces confusion and enhances credibility.

4. **Test and Refine:** Don't guess. Use data to determine what design choices resonate with your audience. Continuously test different elements to see what builds trust and loyalty.

By focusing on these steps, brands can enhance customer trust and ensure their visual identity supports their overall business goals.

35. Strengthening Trust Through Corporate Governance and Compliance

"Ethics is knowing the difference between what you have a right to do and what is right to do."

- Potter Stewart

Jake sat at his desk, reviewing the latest compliance reports, his brow furrowing as he analyzed the numbers. The implementation of Borenstein's GUARDIAN Digital Trust Framework™ had improved some metrics, but he felt there was more they could leverage when it came to governance and compliance.

Just then, Max entered, noticing Jake's intense focus. "You look like you're solving world peace. What's on your mind?" he joked, sitting across from him.

Jake glanced up, offering a faint smile. "Not quite world peace, but maybe a close second for us—corporate governance. The data shows we've made headway with the GUARDIAN Framework, but I want us to be crystal clear on how compliance is shaping our reputation."

Strengthening Trust Through Corporate Governance and Compliance

Max nodded, sensing the weight of Jake's concerns. "GUARDIAN's brought in transparency and trust," he said, "and that's visible. But, as you said, governance isn't just about following rules; it's about people trusting us because we consistently do the right thing, even when no one's watching."

Jake picked up on Max's point. "Exactly. Trust through governance is about showing we're committed to integrity, not just profitability. If we're going to talk about compliance, it's not enough to hit targets. Our entire corporate culture needs to reflect the accountability standards we hold."

Max leaned forward, recalling recent achievements. "The GUARDIAN Framework has given us structure in critical areas—specifically, transparency with our stakeholders and consistent reporting. And it's working. We're seeing an 18% increase in partner confidence scores and a 25% increase in client retention. These numbers are directly tied to our reputation for integrity."

Jake chimed in, "Right. And that's because we've established governance as a real commitment, not just a checkbox. When we share compliance updates with our clients, it's about showing them our accountability. We report on performance, risk management, and ethics just as openly as we report on financials. But there's always room to strengthen that trust, especially around accountability and proactive governance."

Max raised an eyebrow, curious. "Where do you think we're falling short?"

Jake paused, considering his response. "Not necessarily falling short, but we could communicate our policies better, especially internally. For instance, in our data compliance protocols, employees should know exactly why they're there, not just what the rules are. If we want a culture that's truly compliant, we need everyone to understand why compliance isn't just the right thing; it's critical for growth."

"Agreed," Max replied, nodding thoughtfully. "Let's bring in a few more touchpoints with compliance in our onboarding. Transparency from day one can reinforce that compliance is non-negotiable here."

Jake pointed to the data on his screen. "Here's an interesting stat I just found—92% of clients report trust as their main reason for partnering with a vendor, yet nearly 70% have experienced a significant trust breach with at least one partner. That's a gap we can't afford. We need to continue addressing governance with our clients, but we can also put more focus on embedding it into our culture."

Max agreed, "It's all about anticipating and addressing risks before they become problems. With GUARDIAN, we've managed that well. Our increased trust scores show we're on the right path, but to sustain this, we need to ensure our entire team embraces these principles."

Jake added, "Right. And it's not just about having a checklist of rules. It's about a proactive culture that questions, analyzes, and corrects before something goes wrong. Governance has to be an active practice, where we're always looking ahead."

Max, always keen on bringing a vision to life, thought for a moment. "How about implementing regular 'Governance Check-ins'? Quarterly meetings where we go over not only compliance metrics but also examples of where we went above and beyond. This could be an internal culture booster and serve as a powerful external statement about our commitment."

Jake nodded in agreement. "I like that. And we could even extend that into a 'Trust Report' for our clients and stakeholders. Transparency breeds trust, after all."

The two executives continued to strategize, pinpointing how compliance and corporate governance could become even more foundational to Rezilify's culture. The GUARDIAN Framework had proven effective, but they recognized the need to keep evolving.

Craft Your Leadership Trust Strategy:

Jake drew three interconnected circles. "Let's map our governance trust strategy," he began.

Build Trust (Offensive Plays)

"First, we establish governance credibility," he explained:

- Compliance transparency programs
- Corporate governance initiatives
- Stakeholder reporting systems

Protect Trust (Defensive Plays)

Moving to the second circle:

- Compliance monitoring protocols
- Governance risk assessment
- Regulatory tracking systems

Measure Trust

For the final circle:

Trust Metric	Current	Target
Governance Trust	70%	95%
Compliance Score	75%	98%
Stakeholder Trust	68%	85%

"Remember," Jake concluded, "strong governance builds lasting trust."

Steps For the Strategic Leader to Strengthen Trust through Corporate Governance and Compliance:

1. **Embed Compliance in Culture:** Go beyond onboarding training. Offer quarterly governance sessions that cover both compliance and the company's proactive stance on accountability, demonstrating the practical side of these rules.

2. **Proactively Communicate Compliance Measures to Clients**: Develop and share a "Compliance and Governance Report" with key clients. Use it to detail steps taken to meet industry standards, along with updates on risk management practices.

3. **Establish Accountability Touchpoints:** Create a compliance 'check-in' system where each department reviews its adherence to governance principles, looking for ways to go beyond mere compliance. Document and celebrate these examples to strengthen internal culture.

4. **Showcase Compliance Metrics as a Competitive Advantage:** In client pitches and public communications, emphasize trust metrics that highlight governance as part of the company's brand value, such as client retention rates and partner satisfaction scores.

5. **Create a Trust-Building Compliance Scorecard:** Develop a scorecard that quantifies compliance efforts in terms of trust-building outcomes. Measure factors like customer retention, partner confidence, and transparency initiatives and present these regularly to reinforce governance as a measurable asset.

By embracing a proactive approach to compliance and viewing governance as an ongoing journey rather than a one-time task, companies can build a trust-first culture that resonates both internally and externally.

36. Trust, Data Privacy, and the Ethics of AI

"Data is a precious thing and will last longer than the systems themselves."

- Tim Berners-Lee, Inventor of the World Wide Web

After an intense Board meeting on data privacy and the future of AI ethics, Marcella and Jake walked back to the office, replaying the conversations. Rezilify had made strides in both areas, but the Board was pushing them to make privacy and AI ethics integral to their brand, not just as compliance requirements but as central to their values.

Marcella broke the silence. "The Board's message was clear: privacy and AI ethics aren't just about meeting regulations anymore—they're foundational to trust. We have to lead on this, Jake. These aren't boxes we tick; they're core values that need to be woven into our identity."

Jake nodded. "Our data backs it up. Clients are 20% more loyal when they know their data is safe with us. Privacy isn't just a retention tactic; it's a trust issue. And on the AI side, ethics is just as crucial. An ethical, transparent AI framework can be a real differentiator."

As they reached the executive lounge, Kim and Max joined them, with Max looking deep in thought. "Marcella, Jake—our AI ethics discussions just scratched the surface. GUARDIAN gave us a compliance framework, but we're hearing from clients who want more than assurance. They want transparency. They want to know their data won't be exploited by AI or that our algorithms won't unknowingly introduce biases that impact them."

Marcella agreed. "Exactly, Max. Take our privacy promise, for instance. Clients should feel empowered with transparency and control, knowing how their data is used. If data privacy becomes synonymous with Rezilify, it sets a new standard. But it's the same with AI. We need to assure our clients that AI-driven insights are unbiased and responsible."

Kim leaned in. "AI bias is a massive concern. We've seen companies burn trust when AI is perceived as unfair. The Federal Reserve flagged banks' AI lending algorithms last year for disproportionately rejecting minority applicants. Clients need to trust that our AI respects and safeguards their data without unintentionally introducing bias. GUARDIAN can't just focus on security; it has to evolve to cover these new, specific risks."

Max nodded, pulling out his notes from a recent client meeting. "Transparency is key here. If clients understand our AI decisions, especially those that impact them directly, trust grows. Amazon's 2024 transparency model with Alexa's AI decisions— explaining the rationale behind each recommendation—boosted user confidence significantly. That's what we need to aim for."

Jake chimed in. "Data privacy and AI ethics go hand in hand. Privacy isn't just about protection; it's about creating control and giving clients the ability to actively manage their data. And with AI, that means transparency—not just in results but in the process. Imagine if Rezilify could offer a dashboard that details the 'why' behind major AI decisions, from data usage to predictive insights."

Marcella's eyes lit up. "It's time to take this seriously, Jake. We need proactive privacy and AI ethics integrated at every level. GUARDIAN isn't just our safety net; it should be our competitive advantage. Let's build a privacy and AI ethics framework around three pillars: transparency, control, and accountability."

Jake considered this. "And it's more than a risk aversion strategy. Clients are loyal when they know we're safeguarding their data—and acting ethically with it. Research shows that post-breach client churn is at 45% within six months. In AI, unchecked bias could cause just as much damage to trust. This isn't optional—it's a survival strategy."

Marcella drew three interconnected circles on a whiteboard in the lounge. "Here's how we'll build our trust strategy around these ideas," she began.

Craft Your Executive Strategy:

Build Trust (Offensive Plays)

"First, we establish privacy credibility," she explained:

- Data protection programs
- Privacy transparency initiatives
- User control systems

Protect Trust (Defensive Plays)

Moving to the second circle:

- Privacy monitoring protocols
- Data breach prevention
- Compliance verification systems

Measure Trust

For the final circle:

Trust Metric	Current	Target
Privacy Trust	70%	95%
Data Protection	75%	98%
User Control	68%	85%

"Remember," Marcella concluded, "privacy and ethical AI are more than policies. They're the foundation of digital trust, and without trust, we lose clients, credibility, and even our talent."

Steps For the Strategic Leader to Build Trust in the Use of AI:

1. **Establish Transparency and Control**: Develop a clear privacy and AI transparency portal, allowing clients to view and control their data, as well as understand the rationale behind AI-driven decisions.

2. **Position Privacy and AI Ethics as Core Brand Values**: Actively market data privacy and ethical AI as part of the company's commitment to clients, emphasizing that these are non-negotiable values at Rezilify.

3. **Implement Regular Audits for AI Bias and Privacy Protocols:** Conduct frequent privacy checks and AI audits to detect and eliminate bias, reducing ethical risks and improving trust metrics.

4. **Train Teams on Data Privacy and AI Ethics**: Create ongoing training for employees on safeguarding data and ethical AI principles, emphasizing accountability and bias detection in AI algorithms.

5. **Measure and Track Privacy and AI Trust Impact:** Analyze the correlation between

privacy initiatives, AI ethics efforts, and client retention and satisfaction scores. Use these insights to refine policies and reinforce trust.

6. **Communicate Regularly on Privacy and AI Practices:** Send quarterly updates on data privacy measures and AI transparency, highlighting new tools or policies that empower clients to control and understand their data.

By integrating data privacy and ethical AI as core brand elements, Rezilify not only differentiates itself but fosters lasting trust. In a market that increasingly demands transparency and control, companies must balance technological innovation with responsibility, ensuring that trust keeps pace with progress.

37. Using Trust to Build Stronger B2B and B2C Relationships

"Nothing builds trust like the truth, and most customers value truth and honesty above everything else."

- Popular Sentiment

Jake leaned back in his chair, studying the latest report on trust metrics. "These numbers," he murmured as Eric entered, "are really telling a story here."

Eric pulled up a chair across from him. "Talking to your spreadsheet again? I'm guessing it's not all sunshine?"

Jake looked up, intrigued. "Actually, it's fascinating. In 2024, trust has become the primary driver of B2B purchasing decisions—it's even more important than price or product features."

Eric's interest was piqued. "Trust. I know it's been our focus, but that's the needle mover? Can you break it down? What exactly is making them trust us?"

Jake pulled up the key B2B trust statistics on his screen, grounded in the GUARDIAN Framework principles.

Key Trust Metrics

Overall B2B Trust Data:

- 78% of B2B buyers prioritize trustworthiness over price.
- 85% conduct thorough research on a company's reputation before engaging.
- 92% will stop purchasing from a vendor if trust is compromised.
- 67% require third-party validation before making major purchases.

Industry-Specific Trust Insights:

- Technology Sector: Vendor trust (65%), data security confidence (72%), implementation trust (68%), and partner satisfaction (82%).
- Manufacturing: Supply chain trust (58%), quality assurance confidence (75%), delivery reliability (82%), and partner loyalty (76%).
- Professional Services: Expertise trust (71%), project delivery confidence (68%), communication transparency (85%), and long-term relationship trust (79%).

Eric leaned in, seeing the strategic potential. "It stands to reason that if trust is this essential, the financial impact must follow, too. But more so than price or product features? That's quite the eye-opener."

Jake switched to another slide, showing how trust contributes directly to profitability. "Take a look. High-trust B2B relationships don't just create loyalty;

Using Trust to Build Stronger B2B and B2C Relationships

they fuel revenue growth and reduce acquisition costs."

- 23% higher revenue in high-trust B2B relationships.
- 45% faster sales cycles for trusted vendors, accelerating revenue realization.
- 38% increase in customer lifetime value when trust is consistently maintained.
- 25% drop in customer acquisition costs due to the power of referrals.

Eric raised an eyebrow. "That's solid. B2B might seem all about features, but it's trust that keeps clients coming back."

Jake clicked on another slide highlighting the cost of lost trust. "And when trust fails, the metrics tell a much darker story."

- 32% revenue decline following a significant breach of trust.
- 45% increase in customer churn, making retention vital.
- 58% drop in lead conversion rates, putting pressure on sales and marketing.
- Threefold increase in recovery costs as rebuilding loyalty becomes costly.

Eric shook his head. "Imagine trying to win back trust after a major misstep. It's three times harder and way more expensive."

Jake then pointed to the areas where trust investments were paying off, referring back to GUARDIAN's pillars.

Trust Investments That Deliver Returns:

1. Growth Through Authenticity (G):

- Content marketing ROI jumps 35% for trusted brands.
- Event marketing delivers 42% higher response rates with strong trust signals.
- Email open rates improve by 28% due to trust-driven engagement.
- Social media reach expands by 45% for brands perceived as transparent.

2. User Experience Excellence (U):

- Brands that optimize customer experience see engagement and satisfaction rise.

3. Relationship and Brand Management (R, D):

- Account management investments lead to 65% higher retention rates.
- Customer service spending boosts satisfaction by 48%.
- Communication platform ROI improves engagement by 38%.

Jake leaned back, pleased. "The data is clear—consistent investment in these areas reinforces client trust. It's a no-brainer."

Eric nodded. "These are the KPIs we need to keep driving."

Using Trust to Build Stronger B2B and B2C Relationships

Key Performance Targets:

- Partner satisfaction: Target > 85%
- Trust score: Target > 90%
- Implementation success: Target > 95%
- Customer retention: Target > 92%

Expanding the Trust Conversation to B2C:

Just then, Marcella entered and settled in with them both. "I see we're getting detailed on our approach to B2B trust. However, we need to carry that rigor over to the B2C side as well. While B2B is driven by consistency and expertise, B2C trust depends heavily on building emotional connections."

Jake nodded. "For B2C, it's about transparency, control, and engagement." He pulled up some insights grounded in the GUARDIAN Framework:

1. **Authenticity and Transparency (G, T):**

    - 86% of consumers prefer brands that disclose product sourcing and sustainability.
    - 72% of B2C consumers feel more loyal to brands that are transparent about their data usage and privacy policies.

2. **User Experience and Engagement (U, E):**

    - Engaging user experiences leads to 42% higher satisfaction among B2C customers.

- Personalized experiences, like Nike Fit, build trust by demonstrating care for real-life problems.

3. **Community and Emotional Bonds (A, N):**
    - Creating a strong brand community increases retention by 32%.
    - Social sharing and community-driven content can amplify trust by 53% in B2C spaces.

Marcella summarized, "We're looking at creating a brand experience where every interaction feels meaningful. B2C customers need to feel valued, not just informed. That's what builds emotional loyalty."

Jake nodded. "Our trust-building strategy has to go beyond product and service quality—it's about a brand relationship that resonates."

Craft Your Leadership Trust Strategy:

Eric drew three interconnected circles. "Here's our B2B trust blueprint," he began.

Build Trust (Offensive Plays)

"First, we establish B2B credibility," he explained:

- Partner trust programs
- Business relationship systems

Using Trust to Build Stronger B2B and B2C Relationships

- Value delivery protocols

Protect Trust (Defensive Plays)

Moving to the second circle:

- Partnership monitoring
- Relationship verification
- Value protection measures

Measure Trust

For the final circle:

Trust Metric	Current	Target
B2B Trust	70%	90%
Partner Satisfaction	75%	95%
Value Delivery	68%	85%

"Remember," Eric concluded, "B2B trust is built on consistent value delivery."

Steps for the Strategic Leader for Trust Building Stats in B2B and B2C:

B2B Trust-Building

1. Content Marketing: Invest in thought leadership through white papers, webinars, and case studies to educate clients and establish credibility.

2. Transparency: Maintain clear, honest communication. When promises are made, follow through without fail.

3. Digital Presence: Ensure a credible online presence with accurate information, reviews, and testimonials that reinforce buyer confidence.

B2C Trust-Building

1. Emotional Connection: Align the brand with values that matter to consumers, like authenticity and sustainability, and ensure messaging aligns with these values.

2. User-Generated Content: Invite customers to share positive experiences, letting these stories serve as organic trust signals.

3. Loyalty Metrics: Measure trust via customer retention, repeat purchases, and lifetime value, adjusting strategies as necessary.

Using Trust to Build Stronger B2B and B2C Relationships

Across both B2B and B2C, trust remains a continuous effort requiring intentional cultivation at every touchpoint. It's an asset that, when managed well, can yield consistent and measurable returns.

PART VIII: TRUST IN THE FUTURE

38. Leadership Trust in the Digital Era

The hardest thing about leadership is leading yourself. The second hardest is leading others."

— Bill George

Eric and Marcella were in the executive lounge, deep in conversation after another long day of wrangling the complexities of Rezilify's marketing strategy.

"You know what's exhausting?" Marcella said, rubbing her temple. "Navigating this whole 'trust economy.' We're doing a hundred things right, but somehow, it often feels like we're one step behind our competitors."

Eric leaned back on the leather sofa, letting out a frustrated laugh. "Yeah, I hear you. Trust is like quicksand. It's solid when you've got it, but if you don't actively and constantly build on it, you're sinking without even knowing."

Marcella nodded, exasperated. "It's not enough that we're good at what we do. Now, we have to prove we're the trusted experts in the field. That we are the thought leaders. I know we've covered this already. But honestly, half the time, I wonder—who's even deciding what makes someone a thought leader?"

Eric smirked and raised an eyebrow. "Apparently, the ones who shout loudest. We've got the substance, but we're not out there enough. Meanwhile, our competitors are basically hiring megaphones."

Marcella sighed, sinking into her seat. "Exactly. Thought leadership is a crowded space. We've been too quiet with it, and now we're paying for it. Look at how Salesforce managed to own the AI conversation last year. They weren't just pushing their products—they were educating the market. We need to step up in a similar way."

Eric nodded as he sipped his coffee. "Yeah, they turned their marketing into something people actually wanted to read. It wasn't fluff; it was valuable, data-backed content. Even I read them. They weren't just noise. And that's what we need to do."

Marcella sat up straighter, thinking out loud. "Thought leadership has to be more than just marketing. It has to be about real insights and real solutions. That's what will set us apart from all the empty noise out there. The clients that stick with us—they need to see us as their trusted advisors, not just cybersecurity experts."

Eric shook his head and chuckled. "Man, who would've thought saving the world from cyber threats would come down to writing papers and hosting webinars? Philosophers in suits. That's where we're at."

Marcella laughed, though there was an edge of agreement in it. "And who's going to get all that done? Let's be realistic here—we need a solid plan."

Eric pulled out his tablet. "Alright, let's break it down. We're already ahead on trust, but we need to ramp up our visibility as the experts. What do we start with?"

Marcella stood up, pacing the room while she contemplated the options. "Thought leadership content... We need to put out high-quality, research-backed content that showcases our expertise. No fluff, just straight-up insights. IBM did this in 2023 with cybersecurity, and it led to a 35% increase in client retention."

Eric scribbled notes. "Max will love that. He's been dying to turn our messaging into something more impactful. Let's assign him to develop a content calendar—60 days to get the first wave of articles out."

Marcella nodded. "Good. We'll make sure the content addresses emerging cybersecurity challenges, things that keep our clients up at night. And we can back it up with our data and insights."

She paused. "Next up, we need engagement. Webinars, Q&A sessions—anything that gets our clients involved. Salesforce did this beautifully with their AI forums last year. They had thousands of participants, and it solidified their position as thought leaders."

Eric grinned. "That's my wheelhouse. I'll handle the webinars. We can host monthly sessions where we tackle industry trends and challenges. But we need to make it valuable—none of that corporate jargon nonsense."

Marcella smiled. "Perfect. Forty-five days to set up the first one. We can promote it with Max's new content. Clients need to hear directly from us, not just read about what we're doing."

"And Jake?" Eric asked. "Where does he fit in?"

"Data," Marcella said immediately. "He's always talking about how clients want hard numbers, not just opinions. We should partner with a research firm to develop reports that provide real, original insights into cybersecurity trends. Gartner does this all the time, and it gives them credibility."

Eric chuckled. "Jake's gonna love that. Numbers and credibility—he's in his element. Ninety days to get the first report out."

Marcella sat back down, satisfied with the outline. "So, here's the plan: Max handles content, you do the webinars, and Jake backs it all up with data. We turn Rezilify into the go-to voice in cybersecurity."

Eric nodded. "Sounds good. But we're gonna need to keep the momentum going—this isn't a one-and-done deal."

Marcella smiled. "Exactly. We're not just building trust; we're owning the space. And once we do, no one will be able to touch us."

Craft Your Leadership Trust Strategy:

Marcella drew three interconnected circles. "Let's map our leadership trust strategy," she began.

Build Trust (Offensive Plays)

"First, we establish leadership credibility," she explained:

- Digital leadership programs
- Executive transparency initiatives
- Stakeholder engagement systems

Protect Trust (Defensive Plays)

Moving to the second circle:

- Leadership monitoring protocols
- Reputation protection measures
- Crisis response systems

Measure Trust

For the final circle:

Trust Metric	Current	Target
Leadership Trust	70%	95%
Executive Credibility	75%	90%
Stakeholder Confidence	68%	85%

"Remember," Marcella concluded, "digital leadership requires both visibility and authenticity."

Steps for the Strategic Leader to Build Thought Leadership:

1. **Create a Strategic Content Framework:**

    - **Key Content Types:** Focus on valuable, data-backed pieces like white papers, case studies, research reports, and executive perspectives. Ensure content is rooted in solving real client issues.
    - **Content Calendar**: Develop a 60-day calendar that aligns with client needs and industry trends.

2. **Identify Key Distribution Channels:**

    - **LinkedIn:** Utilize it as the primary B2B platform to reach decision-makers.
    - **Industry Publications:** Publish articles in relevant trade magazines and journals.
    - **Email Newsletters & Webinars:** Provide exclusive insights directly to clients and partners.

3. **Implement a Three-Phase Thought Leadership Strategy**:

    - **Phase 1: Foundation (30 Days)** – Form a thought leadership council to identify topics, themes, and target metrics.
    - **Phase 2: Content Creation (60 Days)** – Create flagship content and launch distribution channels, tracking metrics from the beginning.
    - **Phase 3: Optimization (90 Days)** – Analyze early results, refine strategy, and expand distribution based on what's resonating with audiences.

4. **Engage Through Interactive Webinars and Events:**

    - Hold monthly sessions to discuss emerging cybersecurity trends backed by real data and presented in accessible language.

5. **Partner with Research Firms for Credible Data:**

- Work with trusted research firms to release quarterly reports that provide actionable insights, adding data-driven authority to your thought leadership.

6. **Measure Impact Regularly with Key KPIs:**

    - Track metrics like content engagement rates, lead quality improvements, and industry citations.
    - Use trust indicators such as customer feedback, media mentions, and citation frequency to gauge the content's impact.

By following these steps, executives can effectively position their brand as a trusted industry thought leader, providing value through expertise while strengthening long-term client trust.

39. The Role of Ethics in Building Trust

"Ethics is knowing the difference between what you have a right to do and what is right to do."

- Potter Stewart

Jake and Eric met in the quiet of the boardroom after a day of back-to-back meetings, the weight of recent discussions hanging in the air. Jake leaned back, flipping through the day's notes, while Eric tapped his pen thoughtfully against his laptop screen.

Looking up, Jake offered a rare smile. "You know, with all the focus we've put on trust metrics, the ethics piece keeps surfacing as the foundation of it all. Without it, any talk of trust is hollow."

Eric nodded in agreement. "Exactly. Trust doesn't just materialize. Without a strong ethical foundation, there's nothing to build on. We've been approaching trust as if we can engineer it, but it's ethics that make it real. Companies lacking that ethical direction? They're just skating on thin ice."

Jake raised an eyebrow, intrigued. "Without that core, even the best strategies crumble. As we saw with Gen Z and Millennials, today's customers are hyper-aware; they're not just buying a product—they're buying into our values, our approach to privacy, transparency, and accountability. Trust now demands alignment with deeper principles."

Eric leaned forward, his tone more serious. "And it's not just external. Internally, employees need it just as much. They don't just want a paycheck; they want to work for a company that values integrity and respects its people. Without the base of ethical authenticity, our efforts to build internal trust don't hold up."

Jake nodded. "Absolutely. And the impact is twofold. Remember the backlash last quarter after the transparency issues with the leaked emails? It shook team morale, client trust, and even the Board's confidence. That's why ethics can't just be policy; it has to be woven into every decision."

Eric sighed, tapping his pen more thoughtfully. "Right. True integrity doesn't just create trust—it strengthens it over time. Companies that infuse ethics into everything they do don't just build trust; they secure it."

Jake looked at him thoughtfully. "So, how do we keep ethics at the center of every decision? How do we communicate it consistently, both internally and externally?"

Eric paused, then replied, "We need to integrate ethics into decision-making—something actionable, not just philosophical. This is where the GUARDIAN Framework can really come into play."

Applying the GUARDIAN Framework

Growth through Authenticity:

Eric continued, "We should be authentic in every decision, even when it's uncomfortable. That means being transparent about our challenges and our values. We're not just sharing wins; we're creating a space for real conversations with clients and employees. Authenticity builds a trust buffer."

Jake jotted that down. "And authenticity goes both ways. If we're clear and consistent in communicating what we stand for, we're giving our stakeholders—the Board, the team, and our clients—a clear reason to stand by us, even during setbacks."

User-Centric Decision-Making:

Eric added, "Ethics also means seeing decisions through the eyes of those impacted by them. When we think about the client experience and employee morale, it's not just about policies; it's about anticipating the impact on real people. The choices we make should prioritize respect and transparency for both groups."

Jake nodded. "And by keeping user experience at the center, we're aligning decisions with values that build trust, inside and out."

Accountability and Communication:

Eric leaned forward. "Let's formalize a commitment to own our actions. If we communicate openly—especially when things go wrong—it creates trust, not skepticism. Accountability isn't just internal; it's something clients and partners need to see."

Jake wrote down a few notes. "It's also about building a trust buffer, right? When issues arise, if we're already standing on solid ground with our clients and employees, we're not scrambling to rebuild trust—it's already there."

Reliability and Integrity:

Eric continued, "Ethics must go hand-in-hand with reliability. We need to follow through on promises, not just make them. When employees see integrity in practice, they're more motivated to embody it in their work. The same goes for clients—they need to see our integrity reflected in our actions, not just hear it in our words."

Data and Transparency:

Jake nodded. "We can share more than the good metrics. Transparency means letting our stakeholders see the areas where we're aiming to improve. When clients and employees see that, they're more likely to trust that we're genuine."

Inclusivity and Adaptability:

Eric added, "We should include diverse perspectives, especially when addressing ethics. Different viewpoints help us avoid ethical blind spots. And when we're adaptable, we show that we're listening and committed to refining our approach."

Eric leaned back, looking satisfied. "So let's build out specific guidelines that incorporate these steps, with ethics woven into our performance metrics. If we're tracking integrity, transparency, and accountability just as rigorously as financials, we're sending a clear message that ethics isn't optional—it's essential."

Jake nodded. "Agreed. It's time we made ethics a strategic pillar, not just a set of values."

Steps for Building Ethics into Performance Metrics and KPIs

1. **Incorporate Ethics into Evaluation Frameworks:**

    - Establish KPIs tied to ethics and integrity. For instance, track "trust-building actions" or "transparency ratings" in team performance reviews.
    - Monitor ethical decision-making compliance across the company by tracking adherence to ethical guidelines in performance reviews.

2. **Make Ethics a Core Component of Training Programs:**

    - Offer Ethics and Trust Workshops: Develop sessions that train employees on the importance of ethics in client

interactions, data privacy, and transparency.
- Require Ethical Decision-Making Exercises: Create scenarios where employees practice decision-making within the GUARDIAN Framework.

3. **Integrate Ethics into Client and Employee Surveys**:

    - Ask clients and employees to rate the company's transparency, trustworthiness, and ethical integrity in regular feedback surveys.
    - Use this feedback to refine strategies and showcase the impact of ethics-based initiatives in your performance metrics.

4. **Track Progress with a Trust Score:**

    - Establish a Trust Dashboard: Create a dedicated trust scorecard with metrics from all GUARDIAN areas—Growth through Authenticity, Accountability, Reliability, Data Transparency, Inclusivity, and Adaptability.
    - Report on Ethics-Based Metrics Publicly: Share trust and ethics scores with clients and stakeholders. Public reporting reinforces the company's commitment to high ethical standards.

Building an Ethical Culture

1. **Encourage Ethical Leadership at Every Level:**

   - Empower leaders to make ethical decisions and be transparent about the ethical considerations in their decision-making. Highlight leaders who go above and beyond to uphold these values.

2. **Reward Integrity and Ethical Behavior:**

   - Recognize and reward employees who embody the GUARDIAN values. Make ethics a part of performance bonuses, team recognition programs, and other incentives.

3. **Establish a Safe Space for Reporting Ethical Concerns:**

   - Set up anonymous channels for employees to report ethical concerns or breaches. Ensure that they feel safe and supported in bringing these issues forward.

Craft Your Leadership Trust Strategy:

Eric drew three interconnected circles. "Let's map our ethics trust strategy," he began.

Build Trust (Offensive Plays)

"First, we establish ethical credibility," he explained:

- Ethics governance programs
- Transparency initiatives
- Stakeholder engagement systems

Protect Trust (Defensive Plays)

Moving to the second circle:

- Ethics monitoring protocols
- Compliance verification
- Value protection measures

The Role of Ethics in Building Trust

Measure Trust

For the final circle:

Trust Metric	Current	Target
Ethics Trust	70%	95%
Value Alignment	75%	90%
Stakeholder Trust	68%	85%

"Remember," Marcella concluded, "ethical leadership builds lasting trust."

Steps for the Strategic Leader when Defining Ethics:

1. **Growth through Authenticity:**

   - Be Transparent in Communication: Share not only successes but also challenges. When discussing product failures or service shortcomings, be open about the steps being taken to improve.
   - Create Spaces for Real Feedback: Establish regular forums where employees and clients can openly share their experiences.

Listen actively and commit to sincerely addressing their concerns.

2. **User-Centric Decision-Making:**

   - Empathize with Stakeholders: Before making decisions, consider how they will impact employees, clients, and partners. Implement user journey mapping to help visualize these impacts.
   - Prioritize Respect and Privacy: Evaluate policies and practices from a user perspective, focusing on privacy and ethical data usage. Make changes to give users more control over their data, reinforcing trust.

3. **Audience Accountability and Clear Communication:**

   - Own Mistakes and Follow Through When Errors Happen; Take Responsibility: Create a formal process to communicate issues quickly and share updates on the resolution with both internal and external stakeholders.
   - Define Accountability Metrics: Implement metrics that track accountability, such as time to resolution for complaints or issue transparency ratings.

4. **Reliability and Integrity:**

    - Demonstrate Consistency: Track and report on the fulfillment of commitments. Whether it's a client contract or an internal policy, showing consistency in promises builds lasting trust.
    - Integrate Integrity Metrics: Track and reward actions that reflect integrity—such as ethical sales practices, honest communications, and responsible decision-making.

5. **Data and Transparency:**

    - Set Up Transparent Reporting: Regularly report key performance indicators (KPIs) to clients, employees, and stakeholders. Include metrics for areas needing improvement as well as successful outcomes.
    - Educate on Data Handling: Offer regular training sessions on ethical data management and transparency. Make privacy and data ethics part of your ongoing team development.

6. **Inclusivity and Adaptability:**

    - Gather Diverse Perspectives: Include a variety of viewpoints in decision-making. Establish an ethics advisory board or involve representatives from different

departments to bring fresh insights to key decisions.
- Adapt Your Approach Based on Feedback: Show clients and employees that you're committed to change by regularly reviewing policies based on their feedback and adapting strategies as needed.

40. Future Trends in Trust: What Comes Next?

"A trust leap is when we take a risk to do something new or to do it differently from the way that we've done something before."

- Rachel Botsman

Eric was heading out late at the end of the day when he walked past Marcella's office and noticed her still working. He paused, leaning against her door frame with a grin.

"Still burning the midnight oil, huh?" Eric asked.

Marcella looked up from her laptop, smiling. "You know me—never quite done when it comes to figuring out the future."

Eric stepped into her office, curious. "What's on your mind this time?"

Marcella gestured to her screen, where a digital map displayed market trends. "The usual. Trust. How it's evolving and what we need to do to stay ahead of it."

Eric sat down, his interest piqued. "Ah, trust the economy driver. Everyone's talking about it; we've got multiple angles on it, but no one seems to know where it's headed. So, what are we really looking at here? AI? Blockchain? Who's going to standardize the next system of trust?"

Marcella nodded. "All of that—and more. Trust is getting more complicated, and it's not just about what we do now. It's about preparing for what's coming. Emerging technologies, shifting consumer demands, better AI, sustainability … it's all connected. We need to be ready."

Eric leaned back, crossing his arms. "So, what do you think trust will look like five or ten years from now?"

Marcella smiled. "That's what I'm trying to figure out. AI is an obvious big one—consumers are getting more comfortable with it, but that comfort comes with higher expectations. They want transparency. Take Google, for example. They've done a great job being open about how their AI works, like with Google Assistant. People trust them because they explain how it benefits the user and how data is handled."

Eric nodded. "Makes sense. People don't want to feel like they're being blindsided by invisible algorithms."

Marcella agreed. "Exactly. AI is already here, but trust in AI will only grow if companies are clear about how it's used. Then there's blockchain—also a game-changer. It's already transforming industries with its transparency, especially in finance and supply chains."

Eric raised an eyebrow. "Transparency in Blockchain could really shake things up in industries where transparency is sorely lacking—or even avoided."

Marcella chuckled. "That's the point. It's not just a technical breakthrough—it's a shift in how trust is built. Look at IBM. They're using blockchain to let customers track their products from origin to delivery. That kind of transparency is huge for consumers who care about ethical sourcing and sustainability."

Eric leaned forward, intrigued. "And sustainability is only getting bigger, especially with younger generations. If we're not showing a real commitment to it, we risk losing their trust altogether."

Marcella nodded seriously. "Exactly. Companies like Patagonia and Tesla have made sustainability part of their core identity. For Millennials and Gen Z, that's not optional—it's expected. Brands that don't prioritize sustainability are going to get left behind."

Eric sighed. "It's like we're playing a never-ending game of catch-the-carrot-on-a-stick. So, what's the takeaway here?"

Marcella leaned back, her expression thoughtful. "The future of trust is going to be built on three things: technology, transparency, and values. If we want to lead, we have to anticipate these trends—not just react to them. We need to stay ahead of the curve."

Craft Your Executive Strategy:

Marcella drew three interconnected circles. "Here's our future trust blueprint," she began.

Build Trust (Offensive Plays)

"First, we establish future credibility," she explained:

- Emerging technology trust programs
- Future-ready transparency initiatives
- Innovation trust protocols

Protect Trust (Defensive Plays)

Moving to the second circle:

- Future risk assessment
- Technology safety measures
- Innovation protection systems

Measure Trust

For the final circle:

Trust Metric	Current	Target
Future Trust	70%	90%
Innovation Trust	75%	95%
Technology Safety	68%	85%

"Remember," Marcella concluded, "future trust requires present action."

Eric stood up, stretching.

Marcella smiled. "We start by explaining how we're using AI and being transparent about data. We balance that with real human support, and we predict potential problems before they escalate—AI can help with that. And above all, we show that we care about sustainability, not just because it's good for business, but because it's the right thing to do. And by adhering to our GUARDIAN Framework, it lays it out for us; we've already seen how it is applicable in so many scenarios, all we have to do is follow it."

Eric nodded, heading for the door. "Alright, boss. Looks like we've got our work cut out for us. If we can navigate these trends, we'll be in a great position."

Marcella smiled as he left. "Exactly. The future might be complex, but if we understand the trends, we'll be ready to lead."

Steps for the Strategic Leader when Introducing Future Trends:

1. **Explain AI Use:** Make it clear to customers how AI is integrated into your services. Transparency in automation builds trust.

2. **Balance AI with Human Interaction:** While AI can handle efficiency, it ensures customers have the option to connect with a human for personalized service.

3. **Use AI to Predict and Prevent Problems:** Employ AI to forecast potential issues and proactively offer solutions, maintaining trust before challenges arise.

4. **Leverage Blockchain for Transparency:** Adopt blockchain to give consumers a clear view of your processes, especially in areas like supply chain management.

5. **Prioritize Sustainability:** Make sustainability a core value. Consumers, especially younger generations, expect brands to lead on environmental responsibility.

41. Trust and Regulatory Compliance

"Compliance does not foster innovation; trust does. You can't sustain long-term innovation, for example, in a climate of distrust."

— Stephen Covey

Marcella opened the meeting, her expression focused. "Alright, team. Regulatory compliance is becoming essential in building trust with clients and stakeholders. With increasing scrutiny from regulators and heightened expectations, we need to demonstrate that compliance is part of our core trust-building strategy, not just a checklist."

Eric nodded, leaning forward. "The GUARDIAN Framework has already guided us well—especially in areas like Authenticity and Reputation Management. But, regulatory compliance has to be seamlessly integrated into every part of that model. When clients see we're not only compliant but proactive, they trust us more."

Max added, "Right, it's about being proactive, not reactive. Recent feedback shows clients care deeply about data privacy and transparency. They want to know we're committed not just to regulations but to their experience and values."

Jake, focused on numbers, joined in. "Clients are watching, and regulatory fines could hit our bottom line hard if we fall behind. But more than that, reputational damage could cost us long-term trust. Compliance can't be siloed; it has to be a part of our overall trust and growth strategy, especially if we want lasting authority and brand credibility."

Kim nodded. "And this isn't just about clients; it matters to employees, too. Top candidates look for companies that value integrity and transparency. A commitment to compliance reinforces that we're a place people want to work."

Marcella agreed. "Exactly. Compliance needs to be embedded in our GUARDIAN Framework as a core pillar. Accountability, transparency, and adaptability are essential. It's about building resilience, ensuring clarity in who is responsible, and creating a framework where compliance strengthens trust with both our customers and our team."

Eric summed up their thoughts, "If we embed compliance into GUARDIAN's pillars—Growth Through Authenticity, User Experience Excellence, Audience-Centric Analytics, Reputation Management, Digital Brand Authority, Innovative Customer Engagement, Adaptive Marketing Intelligence, and Network Effect Amplification—we'll be fully equipped to manage regulatory demands while building trust."

Marcella motioned for them to dive into each aspect of the GUARDIAN Framework and explore how compliance can be further integrated.

Applying the GUARDIAN Framework to Compliance

Growth Through Authenticity

Eric started, "Authenticity begins with clear, ethical governance. Compliance practices need to be transparent to foster genuine growth. We should openly communicate our compliance measures with clients to show that our commitment to ethics isn't just lip service."

User Experience Excellence

Max added, "Our clients need to feel that compliance enhances, rather than complicates, their experience. Proactively updating them on regulatory practices that affect their data privacy shows that we prioritize their experience and security."

Audience-Centric Analytics

Jake spoke up, "Analytics should track more than performance. We need to incorporate compliance metrics that help us understand and anticipate client concerns. By aligning compliance metrics with audience-centric analytics, we can address client concerns before they escalate."

Reputation Management

Marcella nodded, "Reputation is critical. If we ever face a regulatory issue, we need a proactive approach to manage it. Communicating transparently, acknowledging issues, and detailing solutions reinforce that we're a trustworthy partner, even in challenging situations."

Digital Brand Authority

Kim agreed, "Our brand authority depends on clients seeing us as reliable. A strong compliance framework shows we're leaders in ethical, secure practices, which strengthens our digital brand authority. We need to keep compliance front and center in our brand messaging."

Innovative Customer Engagement

Max chimed in, "We should look for ways to engage clients around compliance—inviting them to co-create ethical guidelines with us, for example, or seeking feedback on our privacy practices. This builds trust through a collaborative approach to compliance."

Adaptive Marketing Intelligence

Jake added, "The regulatory landscape changes constantly. Our compliance systems need to be flexible and able to adjust to new regulations quickly. Integrating compliance monitoring with marketing intelligence ensures we're always one step ahead."

Network Effect Amplification

Eric concluded, "Our clients share information in their networks. If we consistently show we're responsible with compliance, we'll build a positive reputation that amplifies trust. Word-of-mouth is powerful, and proactive compliance boosts that network effect."

Eric drew three interconnected circles. "Here's our regulatory trust blueprint," he began.

Craft Your Leadership Trust Strategy

Build Trust (Offensive Plays)

"First, we establish compliance credibility," he explained:

- Regulatory transparency programs
- Compliance documentation systems
- Stakeholder communication protocols

Protect Trust (Defensive Plays)

Moving to the second circle:

- Compliance monitoring systems
- Regulatory tracking protocols
- Risk assessment measures

Measure Trust

For the final circle:

Trust Metric	Current	Target
Compliance Trust	75%	95%
Regulatory Score	80%	98%
Stakeholder Trust	70%	90%

"Remember," Eric concluded, "compliance builds trust through transparency."

Marcella looked around the table with satisfaction. "We've laid a strong foundation by integrating compliance into GUARDIAN. Let's move forward with these actions, embedding compliance at every level and ensuring it supports both our reputation and our relationships."

Steps for the Strategic Leader to Build Trust Through Compliance:

1. Foster Growth Through Authenticity

- Communicate openly about your compliance framework. Share regular updates on compliance efforts to reinforce authenticity and demonstrate that compliance is core to your growth strategy.

2. Prioritize User Experience Excellence

- Keep clients informed about compliance measures that impact their data and privacy. Show them that regulatory measures enhance their security and overall experience.

3. Use Audience-Centric Analytics

- Integrate compliance metrics into analytics. Track and respond to client concerns around compliance and privacy to show you're proactive and audience-centered.

4. Strengthen Reputation Management

- Build a plan for handling potential compliance issues. Be ready to communicate transparently about challenges and solutions to protect and build your reputation.

5. Enhance Digital Brand Authority

- Position compliance as part of your brand's core. Regularly highlight your commitment to ethical practices in brand messaging and client communications.

6. Engage Customers Innovatively

- Invite clients to participate in compliance discussions. Gather feedback on privacy practices and let them co-create guidelines, demonstrating a collaborative approach.

7. Build Adaptive Marketing Intelligence

- Monitor regulatory changes and integrate them into your marketing intelligence. Ensure that your compliance framework is adaptable and ready to pivot as regulations evolve.

8. Leverage Network Effect Amplification

- Encourage clients to share positive compliance experiences within their networks. Proactive compliance will amplify trust and foster a network of client advocates.

In today's trust economy, regulatory compliance isn't just about adhering to the rules—it's about demonstrating that your organization is ethical, responsible, and dependable. By integrating compliance into a broader trust model, organizations can build resilient, lasting trust with clients and stakeholders alike.

42. Trust in AI-Driven Decision Making

"Automation is good, so long as you know exactly where to put the machine."

— Eliyahu Goldratt

A few days later, Max and Jake found themselves walking together through the hallway, heading to different department meetings. Their conversation naturally drifted to the latest internal discussions about AI and, in particular, the trust issues that had recently surfaced.

Max checked his phone while they walked, glancing up with a puzzled expression. "So, what's this about people losing trust in our AI system?" he asked. "I thought we'd nailed the efficiency part."

Jake adjusted his glasses, nodding. "Efficiency isn't the issue. It's perception. Marcella's been saying that the AI feels too ... cold. Customers are beginning to wonder if the AI's decisions are even fair. And if they start thinking our AI is biased or too detached, it doesn't matter how well it works. We'll lose them."

Max sighed, shaking his head. "We've invested millions to make sure the AI is flawless. What do they expect—personal calls from the CEO every time it makes a recommendation?"

Jake smirked. "Not quite. But they want more than just accuracy. They need to understand the AI's decisions and trust that it's making them responsibly. Transparency is a big part of that."

Max nodded slowly, considering. "So we need to 'humanize' it. But how? We can't explain every decision it makes to every single customer."

Jake paused in front of the elevator, looking thoughtfully at Max. "Actually, we might be able to. Marcella's been talking about Explainable AI. It's a way to show users the logic behind the decisions. Google and a few others are already doing this."

Max raised an eyebrow as the elevator doors opened. "Explainable AI, huh? So, instead of being this mysterious black box, it actually shows people the reasoning behind the choices. But implementing that would take time."

Jake stepped inside and pressed the button for his floor. "True, but Marcella also suggested setting up an appeals process for our AI decisions. It's like customer service for AI—if a customer thinks the AI got it wrong, they can challenge it."

Max leaned against the wall of the elevator, thoughtful. "An appeals process for an algorithm ... I never thought I'd hear those words. But if it'll help rebuild trust, I'm on board. I'll get a team to work on it."

Jake smiled, appreciating Max's willingness to adapt. "And Eric's already working on quarterly bias audits. If people even suspect that the AI is making biased decisions, they'll trust us less. We have to prove that it's fair."

The elevator dinged as they reached Jake's floor. He looked at Max one last time before stepping out. "It's all about transparency, accountability, and fairness. We're not just managing tech here—we're managing trust. Let's make sure our customers feel that this AI is working for them, not against them."

Max nodded as the doors closed. "Right. Time to show them that AI isn't some faceless machine—it's a trustworthy tool they can rely on."

43. Building Trust in AI with Borenstein's GUARDIAN Digital Trust Framework™

As Max and Jake's conversation demonstrates, earning trust in AI involves more than just efficient algorithms. It requires a thoughtful, proactive approach that centers on transparency, fairness, and accountability. To help executives foster trust in AI and other advanced technologies, the GUARDIAN Framework provides a structured approach that addresses key aspects of customer engagement and relationship-building. Here's how each pillar of GUARDIAN can be applied to AI:

G - Growth Through Authenticity

- *Action:* Ensure that AI systems operate transparently, making it clear how and why they make certain decisions. Authenticity requires AI to reflect the values of the organization, demonstrating a commitment to ethical, transparent decision-making.
- *Example:* Publish documentation or case studies that explain how the AI operates and the values it upholds, reinforcing that the system is designed to benefit clients genuinely.

-

U - User Experience Excellence

- *Action:* Prioritize a user-centric approach by integrating Explainable AI features. Allow users to understand and interact with the decision-making process to gain insights into how outcomes are reached.
- *Example:* Incorporate a user-friendly interface that shows customers the factors influencing AI decisions, helping demystify complex processes and reinforcing transparency.

A - Audience-Centric Analytics

- *Action:* Track feedback and user interactions related to AI decisions, especially around issues of fairness and bias. This data can inform future updates and help to promptly address emerging concerns.
- *Example:* Regularly survey users to capture feedback on AI performance, analyzing the results to adjust the AI's parameters or explanations, as needed.

R - Reputation Management

- *Action:* Anticipate potential trust challenges by creating an appeals process, which allows customers to question or review AI-based decisions. When customers see that you're willing to stand by your AI and address issues, they're more likely to trust it.
- *Example:* Establish an "AI Appeals Board" where customers can submit concerns and

Building Trust in AI with Borenstein's GUARDIAN Digital Trust Framework™

receive explanations or alternative solutions, reinforcing accountability and trust.

D - Digital Brand Authority

- *Action:* Position your brand as a leader in ethical AI practices. By demonstrating compliance with the latest standards and implementing regular bias checks, you establish yourself as an authority that clients can trust.
- *Example*: Publicize your regular AI audits and bias testing results, making it known that your brand is dedicated to maintaining fair and responsible AI systems.

I - Innovative Customer Engagement

- *Action:* Engage customers in the AI journey by inviting them to provide feedback or participate in the development of ethical guidelines for AI use. This builds a sense of co-creation and shared responsibility.
- *Example*: Offer a platform where clients can share their AI experiences or concerns, creating a feedback loop that supports trust and engagement.

A - Adaptive Marketing Intelligence

- *Action:* As regulations and technologies evolve, ensure that your AI systems can adapt without compromising trust. Keeping your systems flexible will demonstrate a commitment to responsible, adaptable technology.

- *Example:* Build modular AI systems that can be updated quickly in response to regulatory changes, enhancing both compliance and customer trust.

N - Network Effect Amplification

- *Action:* Foster a community of advocates who trust your AI. Positive experiences with transparent, fair AI will encourage clients to share their stories, amplifying trust across their networks.
- *Example:* Collect testimonials from clients who have benefited from fair and transparent AI decisions, using these endorsements to build a network of trust.

A Final Call to Action

In today's world, trust is no longer an optional part of a successful business, it's a fundamental necessity. Borenstein's GUARDIAN Digital Trust Framework™ isn't just a strategy; it's a mindset that integrates trust-building into every facet of an organization. As Max and Jake discovered, managing AI and other digital tools isn't just about optimizing performance. It's about creating an experience that respects and prioritizes the people it serves.

By humanizing technology, maintaining transparency, and fostering genuine, two-way trust, leaders can ensure their organizations are not only resilient but trusted pillars in the marketplace. The journey to trust may be challenging, but with Borenstein's GUARDIAN Digital Trust Framework™, today's executives have a powerful guide to navigate the digital age—fostering meaningful, lasting relationships with both customers and employees alike.

Let this be the beginning of a new era of trust— one where companies, leaders, and technologies work together to build a brighter, more connected, and more trustworthy future.

EPILOGUE:
The Trust Imperative - What Comes Next?

As we wrap up our journey through the digital trust frontier, one thing has become glaringly obvious: trust is not some shiny trophy you win and display on a shelf. Nope, it's more like a houseplant—if you don't water it, it withers, and trust me, no one wants to deal with those sad, wilted leaves.

Keeping trust alive is a process, a constant balancing act between innovation and transparency and between automation and authenticity.

If there's one lesson we can take from following the adventures of Rezilify's C-suite team, it's this: trust in today's world isn't static. It's a fluid, ever-evolving force that touches every corner of your business.

It's easy to talk about how important trust is, but the real challenge is living it, day in and day out. And in a world dominated by algorithms and automation, where every buzzword from "blockchain" to "AI ethics" seems to promise salvation, trust is quickly becoming the defining factor between success and failure.

So, what now? Where do we go from here?

Trust Through Innovation

We've seen firsthand how innovation—when done right—can be a powerful trust-builder. AI, blockchain, and decentralized platforms aren't just cool tech buzzwords anymore. They're tools to foster transparency and boost customer confidence. But here's the catch: innovation without integrity is just fancy window dressing. If you're not using these technologies in a way that actually benefits your customers (and explaining how they do), you're missing the point.

The Future of Transparency

Transparency isn't optional anymore; it's expected. Customers want to know everything—how you're using their data, where their products come from, and whether you really mean it when you say you're "ethical." They don't want to be dazzled by smoke and mirrors. They want clarity. If that makes you nervous, good—it should. Whether it's real-time data dashboards, explainable AI, or publishing supply chain details for all to see, openness is now a key to survival. If you're still thinking about transparency as an optional feature, it's time for a wake-up call.

Trust in Human Relationships

Here's something refreshing: despite all the AI and automation flying around, human relationships still matter. In fact, they're more important than ever. Brands that manage to blend efficiency with empathy and balance automation with a real human touch will be the ones that come out on top. We might be living in a digital world, but trust is still built person-to-person—even if that person is behind a chatbot (that's programmed with some actual empathy).

The Trust Imperative – What Comes Next?

The Trust Economy

We are officially in the age where trust is the most valuable currency, and no, I don't mean a quirky new cryptocurrency. The companies that get this will prioritize customer experience, privacy, transparency, and ethics. Those that don't? Well, they'll be left scrambling to catch up while the rest of us sit back and enjoy the benefits of being proactive. In the end, trust isn't something you just add to your business strategy—it is its very foundation.

Looking Ahead

If there's one takeaway from this book, it's that trust is never "done." It's a moving target, shaped by new technologies, shifting customer expectations, and evolving social dynamics. So, as we look to the future, the question isn't just "What are you doing today to build trust?" but "How are you preparing for tomorrow's challenges?" Because let's face it—there will always be new crises, new tech trends, and new ways for things to go sideways. The brands that stand out will be the ones that treat trust as an ongoing commitment, not a box to check off.

So, as we stand on the brink of this ever-changing landscape, ask yourself: Are you ready to adapt? To stay ahead of the curve, not just in tech but in trust? Because the future of business isn't just about what you sell; it's about the confidence people have in what you stand for.

And there it is—the future of trust is here, and it's your job to make sure you don't end up with a dead houseplant on your hands. Embrace it, nurture it, and watch your business thrive in ways you never thought possible.

MLA Bibliography

1. Berners-Lee, Tim. "The World Wide Web: A Very Short Personal History." W3C, 1998, www.w3.org/People/Berners-Lee/ShortHistory.html.

2. Borenstein, Gal. *The GUARDIAN Digital Trust Framework: Building Trust in a Digital World.* AMHERST & YALE Publishing, 2024.

3. Brown, Thomas. "Federal Reserve Issues 2023 AI Bias Warning to Banks Over Lending Algorithms." *Financial Regulatory News,* 28 Sep. 2023.

4. Cialdini, Robert B. *Influence: The Psychology of Persuasion.* Revised ed., Harper Business, 2007.

5. Clarke, Emily, ed. "Adobe's AI Marketing Tools Drive 55% Traffic Surge." *Digital Marketing Journal,* 5 May 2023.

6. Covey, Stephen M.R. *The Speed of Trust: The One Thing That Changes Everything.* Free Press, 2006.

7. GuideWire. https://www.guidewire.com/resources/blog/technology/the-financial-impact-of-the-crowdstrike-global-it-outage

8. Davis, Rachel. "Starbucks Enhances Transparency with New Sourcing Program." *Coffee Industry Journal,* 20 Mar. 2024.

9. Edelman, Richard. "2023 Edelman Trust Barometer." Edelman, 2023, www.edelman.com/trust/2023-trust-barometer.

10. Federal Trade Commission. "Consumer Sentinel Network Data Book 2022." FTC, Feb. 2023, www.ftc.gov/reports/consumer-sentinel-network-data-book-2022.

11. Harris, Kamala D. "https://oag.ca.gov/news/press-releases/attorney-general-kamala-d-harris-issues-consumer-alert-warning-california

12. Harris, Samuel. "Mayo Clinic's Patient Trust Framework Elevates Patient Satisfaction by 38%." *Healthcare Today,* 2 Feb. 2024.

13. Hootsuite. "The Global State of Digital 2023." Hootsuite, 2023, blog.hootsuite.com/digital-2023/.

14. Johnson, Laura. "Patagonia's Ethical Sourcing Transparency Sets New Standards Amid Crisis." *Sustainability Report,* 1 Mar. 2024.

15. Lee, Andrew. "Nike's Trust Score Initiative Boosts Online Sales." *E-commerce Times,* 5 June 2024.

MLA Bibliography

16. McKinsey & Company. "The Business Value of Design." McKinsey & Company, Oct. 2018, www.mckinsey.com/business-functions/mckinsey-design/our-insights/the-business-value-of-design.

17. Meta. "2023 Privacy and Transparency Initiatives." Meta, Apr. 2023, about.meta.com/transparency-initiatives

18. Mitchell, Ann, ed. "Amazon's 2024 Transparency Policy with Alexa Enhances User Trust." *Tech Innovation Weekly,* 10 Apr. 2024.

19. Moore, Lucy. "Amazon's Customer Trust Program Drives 25% Increase in Repeat Purchases." *E-commerce Innovations,* 22 Feb. 2024.

20. Morning Consult. "The Power of Influence: Why Gen Z Consumers Trust Social Media Influencers." Morning Consult, 2023, https://pro.morningconsult.com/analysis/influencers-content-creators-evolving-power-2024

21. OpenAI. Open AI Made 5 Huge Governance. Yahoo Finance-Fortune: https://finance.yahoo.com/news/openai-made-5-huge-governance-200942348.html

22. Pew Research Center. "Social Media Fact Sheet." Pew Research Center, April 2021, www.pewresearch.org/internet/fact-sheet/social-media/.

23. Porter, Michael E., and James E. Heppelmann. "How Smart, Connected Products Are Transforming Competition." *Harvard Business Review,* Nov. 2014, https://hbr.org/2014/11/how-smart-connected-products-are-transforming-competition

24. PwC. "Consumer Intelligence Series: Protect.me." PwC, 2017, www.pwc.com/us/en/services/consulting/cybersecurity/library/consumer-intelligence-series.html.

25. Rodriguez, Miguel. "Coca-Cola Announces 100% Recyclable Packaging Goal." *Environmental News Network,* 10 Jan. 2024.

26. Simmons, Eric. "Microsoft's Trust Measures Lead to 28% Metric Increase." *Tech Trust Weekly,* 20 July 2024.

27. Smith, Aaron. "Public Attitudes Toward Computer Algorithms." Pew Research Center, Nov. 2018, www.pewresearch.org/internet/2018/11/16/public-attitudes-toward-computer-algorithms/.

28. Statista. Worldwide digital population 2024 https://www.statista.com/statistics/617136/digital-population-worldwide

29. Statista. "Impact of Fake Online Reviews on E-commerce Spending in the U.S." Statista, 2024, www.statista.com/statistics/fake-online-reviews-ecommerce-impact-us/.

30. Inevspcro. Vergara, Juliana. "Trust is a currency; you can't afford not to invest in it." *Altus Growth Partners Insights,* 2024. https://www.invespcro.com/blog/fake-reviews-statistics/

31. Walters, Laura, ed. "Adobe's Trust Strategy Cuts Response Time by 65%." *Customer Service Today,* 10 Sept. 2024.

32. White, Hannah. "Adidas Launches Custom Sneaker Line to Boost Engagement." *Footwear News,* 5 Feb. 2024.

33. World Economic Forum. "The Global Risks Report 2023." World Economic Forum, 2023, www.weforum.org/reports/global-risks-report-2023.

END

Don't Believe the Hype

To contact the author, Gal Borenstein, reach out by

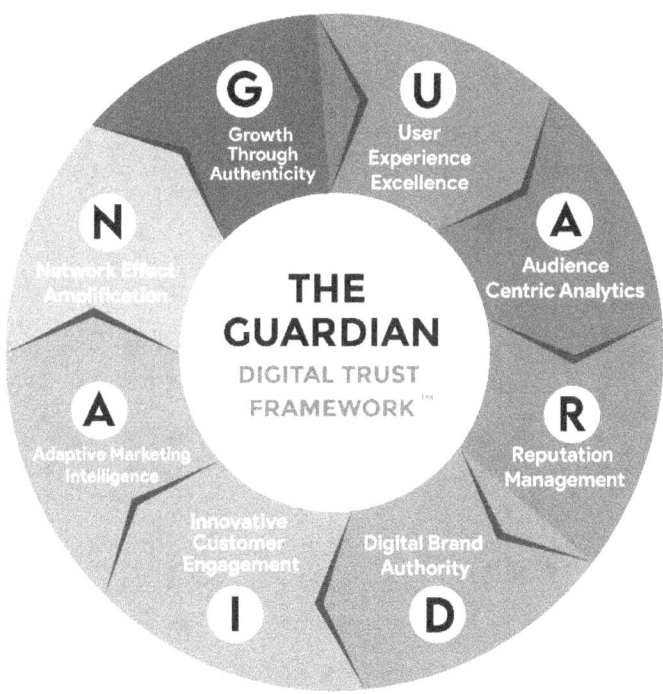

email: Gal@BorensteinGroup.com or via phone: 703-597-1610.

www.ingramcontent.com/pod-product-compliance
Lightning Source LLC
Chambersburg PA
CBHW032210220526
45472CB00018B/653